Angling Afloat

ANGLING AFLOAT

A Complete Guide for Coarse Fishermen

Stephen Harper

The Crowood Press

First published in 1989 by
The Crowood Press
Ramsbury, Marlborough
Wiltshire SN8 2HE

British Library Cataloguing in Publication Data

Harper, Stephen
    Angling afloat: a complete guide for coarse fishe-
    1. Boating manuals. For angling
    I. Title
    797.1'02'47991

    ISBN 1–85223–205–6

To my father, Leslie C. Harper, who first taught me of the pleasures in angling afloat
Line-drawings by the author.

Typeset by Jahweh Associates, Stroud.
Printed in Great Britain by The Bath Press.

Contents

Preface

To some extent, the list of contributors to this book reads like a *Who's Who* of many of today's leading specialist anglers. They all have extensive knowledge in their particular field, indeed most are all-round anglers with knowledge spanning many different species, waters and types of angling. They all fish for 'coarse' fish but their methods and tackle are far from being coarse in any way.

This book is concerned with the capture from boats of these so-called 'coarse' species of fish, an unfortunate term that has been derided by many eminent anglers including Richard Walker.

Boats, in their many forms, have always played a vitally important role in coarse angling in this country. It is doubtful that any serious angler today could pursue his chosen sport without, at some point, fishing afloat and experiencing its delights and dangers.

The anglers of this country are extremely fortunate in the richness, diversity and history of their angling literature. From the very first angling books to the present day, all aspects of our intricate sport have been covered in great detail. Boats and boat fishing have regularly been mentioned in sections of books and have sometimes been given a full chapter, but I am unaware of them being the subject of a complete book dedicated to coarse angling. I am sure this volume will go a long way towards rectifying this omission.

Stephen Harper
Old Costessey, Norfolk
January 1989

Acknowledgements

I would like to thank all the angling writers who have contributed to this book. Without exception, they offered their expertise and advice with great enthusiasm and professionalism.

I would also like to thank my mother, Mrs Freda Harper, who typed a great deal of the manuscript, often at very short notice.

Introduction

Fishing from a boat – to some anglers it is heaven, to others it is hell. Either way, if you are a serious angler in pursuit of many of the coarse species available in the British Isles the day will come when, out of necessity, you will have to leave dry land and take to the water to pursue your chosen species.

I regard myself as fortunate in that I greatly enjoy boat fishing and all that goes with it. It can be almost as pleasurable as catching fish and certainly enhances the enjoyment of angling. As Ratty said in Kenneth Grahame's *Wind in the Willows*,

There is nothing – absolutely nothing – half so much fun as simply messing about in boats. Simply messing . . .

Apart from fishing, that is! This enjoyment is even greater if the boat is your own, reliably customised and adapted to your requirements and needs. Not having to rely on hire boats, or being prepared for them if you do, is paramount and the first rule of boat fishing after safety.

It is something very special to be on the water with the freedom to choose your swim almost without restriction – no problems with moving swims, or carrying tackle around the lake only to find someone already in your intended swim. With boats it's just a matter of reeling in, raising the anchors and moving on to another area. Everything is so convenient, compact and close to hand.

Afloat you can be much nearer to your quarry, even directly above it, but you are also at the mercy of the elements, a small vulnerable capsule of civilisation on a vast sheet of sometimes wild water. The basic safety rules must always be observed and a modicum of common sense is a useful asset. After all, angling is only a hobby and should always be enjoyed rather than endured. To risk life and limb to catch a fish is not only foolhardy but totally insane. Not all eventualities can be foreseen, however, and being prepared and knowing what to do at a critical moment may possibly save your life.

Boats and angling have always been closely linked. The first man to take to a boat was probably a fisherman – if not an angler – and the first boats were almost certainly fishing boats. This link is confirmed much later by the earliest known illustration of a fishing reel, a thirteenth-century Chinese illustration by Ma Yuan. The angler is shown with a very short rod and a reel and is fishing from a boat. (Note the vogue for short boat rods even then!)

In Britain, boat fishing has always been popular and, at certain times, even fashionable. During the nineteenth and the early twentieth century, men in striped blazers and boaters would 'scratch' for gudgeon from elegant punts whilst their lady folk prepared wonderful picnics enjoyed beneath the weeping willows along the banks of the Thames and other English rivers. The one-time English record pike of thirty-seven and a half pounds was taken from a punt on the Hampshire Avon in 1944 by Clifford Warwick and illustrates the good use to which these craft were put until their popu-

Fig 1   The earliest-known illustration of a fishing reel from a Chinese painting by Ma Yuan, and the angler is boat fishing!

larity waned just after the Second World War. Wonderful catches were made, including some incredible hauls of fish of other species, when our rivers held vast shoals and suffered little from pollution and overfishing.

As the twentieth century moved into its second half, with leisure time becoming more available to the average working man, angling became increasingly popular and began to be taken more seriously by a new breed of thinking angler. No sporting species was given any peace from their attentions and the remotest parts of the remotest waters in all areas of the British Isles became their hunting grounds, often with the extensive use of boats.

The pioneers were the pike and trout fishermen, who have developed boat fishing into a new art and have devised new methods, gadgets and accessories to make boat fishing a safer, more enjoyable and more efficient pastime. In America, Holland and other countries, anglers have taken this even further and their custom-built boats must be seen to be believed. Designed specifically for anglers, their features include flat decks, weather canopies, bait wells, swivel chairs, separate trolling motors and a plethora of other built-

in extras. To some degree they put our British boats to shame, but things are developing all the time and, as British anglers travel further afield in search of those elusive monsters, ideas are brought back, adapted and even improved upon. Most of the other species have, at some time or another been tackled from afloat. Roach, chub, tench, bream, even carp and barbel and most of the less popular species can and have all been caught by boat anglers.

The advantage gained from boats is obvious and can be summed up in two words: mobility and accessibility. From a canoe on a small river, trotting for roach, to a wooden clinker-built sea-going rowing boat on the vastness of a Scottish loch, the purpose is the same – to get the angler to the fish. The restrictions circumscribing the bank angler are innumerable – inaccessible banks, overhanging trees, a shallow margin round the perimeter of any water as wide as the longest cast or drift, even if the wind is co-operative. Once afloat, there is no need to cast great distances. It is easier and more effective simply to move the boat!

There is no substitute for a boat and results can sometimes improve dramatically when the angler leaves the bank and searches out his quarry at closer quarters. With the advent of depth and fish finders, boat fishing has been brought well and truly into the space age and has come a very long way since the first true angler took rod and reel aboard a boat and escaped from the confines and restrictions of the bank side.

If the advantages of fishing from a boat are legion, the disadvantages can sometimes run them a close second – but to my mind are finally outweighed. The sometimes unstable and confined nature of boats can be dangerous, but with careful planning and fanatical tidiness this can be alleviated to some degree. The main enemy of the boat angler, and one that can in no way be controlled, is the weather. Always be prepared for any eventuality and if in doubt – leave it out! There is always tomorrow to catch that monster.

PART 1

Basics and Beyond

HIRING A BOAT

If you are considering hiring a boat, and in some situations this is unavoidable, then be prepared for the basic necessities either not to be included in your hire or to be non-operational if they are included. Anchors may be non-existent or inadequate for the job in hand, especially if strong winds are expected. Anchor cables will probably be too short, full of knots and often not even tied to the boat.

Some boats are hired out half full of water, so take a bailer with you. Even oars can sometimes be a problem. It's handy to have your own set in the car in case of emergencies. There's nothing worse than waiting for the boat-yard to open to collect the oars, or spending a windy day in a boat with unsuitable oars or no oars at all.

Spare rowlocks are another item that can always be carried. They don't take up much room and are not heavy. To be marooned with only one rowlock in the middle of a large lake or broad as night closes in isn't much fun, though tying the oar into the hole left by the absent rowlock will usually get you back to shore and safety.

Some boat-yards have finally begun to supply old pieces of carpet for the boat wells to protect the fish, but this is still rare. It is therefore advisable always to take your own. Better to be safe than sorry.

Hire charges can range from as little as £2 per day if you are a member of a club with boats up to around £7 per day. The prices on trout reservoirs are in a different league, £15–£20 per day not being unheard of, so enquire first and take your cheque book.

If you do use a boat-yard that does hire out clean, baled boats with adequate anchors and cables, think yourself a lucky angler. Most boat users would not grudge paying a little extra for good service but it goes against the grain to pay over the odds for unserviced and inadequate hire craft.

BUYING A BOAT

Before you even consider buying a boat it is best to have some experience of boats and boat fishing to know what you are looking for. If you don't feel confident, ask the advice of an experienced boat angler and above all take into consideration the type of fishing the boat will be doing and on what types of water. The boat does not exist that is ideally suited to all waters and forms of fishing. A flat-bottomed punt, suitable for the broads or a slow river, will be next to useless on an Irish lough.

A boat need not be expensive and it is usually financially advantageous to buy second-hand, especially with fibreglass boats. Prices for a second-hand dinghy of 10–13 feet can range from £50 to £300, depending on your budget, quality and the type of boat you are after.

Costs can be kept down if you club together with friends. This is a very popular way to buy boats in Norfolk and means that a group of friends can have several boats all moored at different locations around the

Several different types of club boat moored on a Norfolk broad.

broads. For one boat, two people is obviously the best number. Three and four and it can get complicated, everyone wanting to fish on the same day, usually at weekends!

Bargains can be found in the classifieds of the local press at the right times of year but you will usually have to be pretty quick off the mark as they are snapped up very fast. In Norfolk we are lucky. We are close to the coast and broads, and boat sales are held at certain times of the year. A bargain can be picked up if you are lucky enough to be in the right place at the right time – with the right money. If possible, buy the boat, trailer and lighting bar all at the same time. It is almost impossible to buy a reasonably cheap trailer on its own. Should you intend to transport your boat on the car roof the problem does not arise, but make sure you have a good sturdy set of ladder racks. Most car roof racks are not strong enough.

The two main boat-building materials are obviously wood and fibreglass. Occasionally

I have seen metal boats, usually aluminium, but I have little experience of them – though it does seem that they act as a sounding-board to even the slightest noise.

I prefer to fish from wooden boats. They are vastly superior to fibreglass with regard to stability. A wooden boat tends to sit *in* the water; a fibreglass boat sits *on* the water. Wooden craft make for a much better fishing platform than fibreglass, which can be very unstable, especially those with steeply curving hulls. In a small fibreglass dinghy it can seem as if you're fishing from a plastic washing-up bowl, although one of those would probably be much more stable!

My ideal fishing boat, not suited to wild waters, is the old traditional punt, but with streamlined or scooped bows to allow for easier rowing. These punts are very stable, they displace only inches of water and so can be taken into the shallowest of areas, and their vertical sides mean that no deck area is lost: the ideal fishing platform. The only

A typical fishing punt.

problem with the larger punts is their un-gainliness. Some are almost unrowable and it feels as if you are trying to push them through thick mud. I hate to think what they are like in a headwind.

On the minus side, wooden boats are much heavier than fibreglass ones and there-fore much more difficult to transport. They need constant maintenance and a complete coat of varnish or paint at least once every two years or rot will soon set in. Fibreglass boats are now much more popular for that very reason and wooden boats are gradually becoming rarer. Fibreglass requires little or no maintenance, is very light to transport and can be very cheap. Many fibreglass boats also have the added advantage of built-in buoyancy tanks.

TRANSPORT

The cheapest way to transport your boat to the waterside is on the car roof. A sturdy set of ladder racks will cost about £15–£20. The only other requirements are a few lengths of

rope and some muscle power to get the boat on and off. A 10- or 12-foot fibreglass or wooden dinghy will usually need two people to manhandle it, so if you are planning a day alone in your boat you can be faced with a problem.

This can be overcome with the use of two wooden 'crutches' with a metal shelf bracket bolted on midway and tied at an angle to the ladder racks. With these, one man can get a reasonably big boat on and off a car roof by following the procedure shown in the photographs.

1 One end of the boat is rested on the first bracket.
2 The other end of the boat is rested on the other bracket.
3 The boat is lifted and, with its full weight now resting on the ladder racks, it is slid into position and tied on.

To get the boat off, the procedure is simply reversed.

A garage can also be a great help. By means of a supporting cradle on pulleys

One end of the boat is rested on the first bracket.

from the rafters of the garage, the boat can be lowered directly onto the car roof. At the end of an outing the car can be driven into the garage beneath the cradle. The boat is then tied in and hoisted up. The advantage of this method is the storage of the boat in the otherwise wasted roof space of most garages.

If your boat is very heavy or very large, then there is no alternative to a trailer. Trailers, with their accompanying extras such as tow-bar, lighting bar and winch, can sometimes add up to more than the price of the boat itself, but they are more convenient and solve many of the problems, especially if you are launching single-handed.

TO MOOR OR NOT TO MOOR

Very often, boats can be moored on river, canal and even some stillwaters at little or no

Moving to the other end of the boat, that too is rested on the other bracket.

The boat is raised with its full weight now resting on the ladder racks and is slid into position.

The boat in position on the car roof.

A moored boat with an ample supply of rain-water (the grass is an optional extra!)

cost. The advantages of this are obvious. No worries about transport or manhandling the boat before a fishing trip. Just jump in and away you go!

It is wise, however, to consider the disadvantages. Wooden boats, if left in the water for too long, will inevitably take in water where paint or varnish has been removed. Fibreglass does not suffer from this problem but both types are open to vandalism and even theft. Most moored boats are secured with a stout chain and padlock but even this will not deter a determined thief.

Boats will also have to be visited regularly even when not in use, simply to be bailed out. If left, the rain-water will build up and eventually sink them and it is no easy matter to retrieve a submerged boat, especially if it has sunk into thick mud. This I recently found out after reclaiming a fibreglass dinghy that Martyn Page and I had neglected for over two months on the River Bure. In Scotland, the game anglers solve these problems effectively by mooring out in the lochs to deter vandalism and using a supported boat cover so their boats are always protected from rain-water.

The other main disadvantage of mooring is being restricted to one water if you have only one boat. If you use a trailer or the car roof, your options are left wide open and you can choose the fishing location on the day, taking into account weather conditions and the pattern that angling has taken recently on your intended waters. It's no good having a wonderful boat moored on a water all season when everything is happening elsewhere!

BOATCRAFT

Boatcraft is a very difficult thing to define as it encompasses all aspects of being afloat.

The boats of Scottish game anglers covered to protect against the elements and moored away from the bank to deter vandalism and theft.

Some anglers have it naturally, others have to learn it the hard way and some never seem to master it at all!

One very important aspect is organisation and tidiness. Everything should have its place, be close at hand and be returned there after use. Tackle is best reduced to an absolute minimum and stored in small bags that can easily be tucked away below seats, in cubby-holes or compartments. Large boxes, baskets and rucksacks should be avoided if at all possible, as should fold-up chairs, which can be noisy and even dangerous in some boats. The main area of deck space should be left completely free as an unhooking area for both anglers.

Once the gear has been stashed about the boat logically and tidily, everything should be made ready for fishing before you set out from the bank. Make sure that the anchor cables are free and long enough for your intended swim. Once you reach it, if there is

even a moderate wind and the anchors are not lowered at the right moment you will miss the area and will have to approach it again from downwind, possibly disturbing any fish in residence.

Rods and landing nets should be set up and checked *before* you set out. Bait boxes, bags and anything that will be needed should be made ready and accessible. All this will help to keep down noise and vibrations in the swim, which could scare any fish in the immediate vicinity, especially the wisest and largest of the shoal.

Extra-special care must be taken in approaching the swim and anchoring. If using a motor, turn it off well before the swim is neared and row the last hundred yards or so. Many anglers forget this simple point and seem unable to move a boat any distance at all, even in a flat calm, without starting the motor. Some people's rowing probably makes more of a commotion than

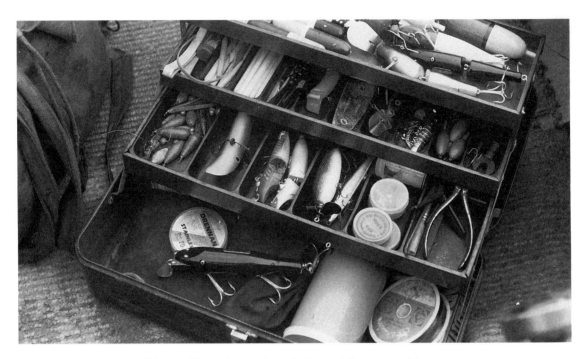

Tackle is best stored in small bags and boxes that can be stashed away below seats and in cubby-holes.

Tackle and accessories should always be kept to the bare minimum!

an engine anyway!

Should a boat's rowlocks be at all noisy, they should not be used for the final stages of approaching a swim. Paddle the boat slowly and quietly with an oar until the anchor point is reached and then lower the anchors slowly and gently, ensuring that they are not bumped on the boat in the process. It cannot be overstressed that it is impossible to be too quiet in a boat. Many fish never see the angler's bait, having been scared off long before the first cast is made.

Once you are anchored and fishing, all movement should be slow and controlled. Anything that can cause noise and therefore vibration must be avoided to ensure that fish can be attracted into the immediate area and, once there, encouraged to remain and feed confidently. This area, defined by the casting range round the boat, should be an area attractive to fish, one that they are not

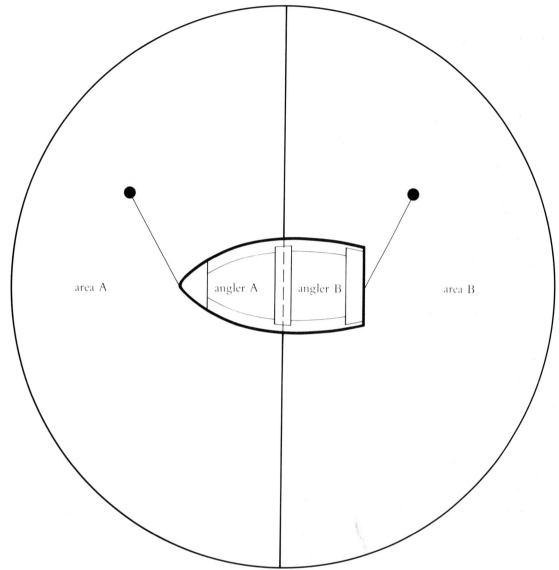

area A   angler A   angler B   area B

Fig 2 The 'half boat' rule.

wary of – not an area where they will be uneasy and soon shy away from.

The subject of the casting area round a boat leads me to the 'half boat' rule for two anglers. An imaginary line drawn across the beam of the boat (or from bows to stern) halves it and extends out across the water on either side. This line should not be cast across by either angler, thereby avoiding tangles and disputes. This rule should be broken only by agreement, in unusual or extreme situations.

Having emphasised so strongly the need for quietness when approaching and fishing a swim, I should perhaps mention that there is one exception to this golden rule. That exception is when the fish have to be stirred or moved into feeding! (This does, however, apply mainly to the predatory species.) On many occasions I can remember when this tactic has worked and worked dramatically after a very slow start. It was in 1971 that I first observed someone using this method and it illustrated to me in a very graphic way how effective it can be. I am still not sure whether it was intentional or not but it certainly worked.

In a certain well-known very shallow and very weedy bay on Loch Lomond in early summer many seasons ago three friends and I had enjoyed many hours of fishing, fighting some epic battles with pike large and small. This was our last morning and we had begun to consider ourselves as instant experts. We scoffed as one boat chugged its way into the bay with engine running constantly until it almost ran full pelt into the weed along the far bank. The boat was still moving into the weed as the two anchors made their deafening entries into the water, shattering what was left of the calm morning as thumps and bangs added to the confusion. How anyone could expect to catch after this performance was beyond us, but the old man and his son seemed undeterred and began to fish, their boat sitting in the weed and their baits cast out into the clear water.

After fishing since dawn, the time came when we had to reel in from the last cast and make our way back to the boat-yard and finally homeward. As we left the bay we noticed, in the distance, the old man standing, his rod well arched against the skyline and his son poised ready with the net. We carried on unimpressed, agreeing amongst ourselves that it could at best be only a small double after we had already fished the area and all the commotion of their arrival. Just before we left for home we learnt the true weight of that fish: thirty-one pounds twelve ounces. Whether by accident or – more likely – by design, the old man had flushed a monster from its sanctuary within the weed bed and succeeded in the very area where our conventional tactics had caught only smaller pike.

It was a lesson well learnt and since that day I have used this tactic to good effect on several occasions, shocking other anglers firstly with the commotion and secondly with the fish! Knowing when to use a softly, softly approach and when to adopt more drastic measures is one more facet of boat-craft. (It should be added that a strong wind can often have a similar effect on some waters after a prolonged settled period.)

SAFETY FIRST

Boat fishing, even if you can swim, can be dangerous on almost any water in the wrong conditions. I often wonder as I head off alone into the vast wilds of somewhere such as the Thurne system what would happen if I ran into trouble. No one knows where I have gone or when I will be back. The only other people I will see in the depths of winter will probably be other anglers.

So, if on my own and in trouble, I would have to rely on my boatcraft, common sense and good luck to see me through. It is advisable therefore, always to inform someone of your intended whereabouts and to take a basic first-aid kit along just in case. Minor accidents, such as a meeting with a pike's teeth, can often occur during a day afloat and I know of at least two instances when hospital treatment followed incidents involving treble hooks.

The first occurred in the heat of a a very successful piking session. A twenty pounder and several double-figure pike had been boated and another very large fish lost at the net. A suspect trace had been discarded in all the excitement and left on a seat. All was well until the boat rocked and the angler stumbled. He put out his hand to break the fall, right on the insidiously placed treble hook. One arm of the treble went in so deep below the thumb that as we tried to retrieve it, the tendons in the forearm were seen to move!

We decided then to leave it to the experts and the hook was finally removed at the Norfolk and Norwich Hospital.

The second incident happened as the result of a casting accident. Nowhere do anglers fish so closely as in the restricted space of a small boat. Special care must be taken when casting any baits, but especially large pike baits with their attendant treble hooks. The wise angler always wears some form of headgear as even a light hat can deflect the hooks of a miscast. Unfortunately, on this occasion the victim was bareheaded, and, as the herring was aimed at the horizon with great power by his boat partner, the hooks found a home prematurely in his unprotected scalp. The line parted with the crack of a pistol shot as a whelp and a curse echoed across the Broadland landscape. Several would-be scalp surgeons tried their best with forceps to extract the offending barbs between screams but eventually they had to admit defeat and much later the unfortunate angler was wheeled into Great Yarmouth Infirmary with trace and herring still in place. The nurses were much more amused than the unfortunate angler!

But the main safety concern is always the weather. Many of the smaller or enclosed waters never suffer greatly from the effects of wind but the larger, more exposed waters are often at the mercy of the elements. Very early during my boating adventures I experienced weather conditions on Loch Lomond the like of which I have not seen before or since. That day instilled in me a very healthy caution and respect for the weather whilst afloat and is perhaps best illustrated by the story itself.

BEWARE THE WHITE HORSES

As the two boats set out from the wooden jetty, one towing the other, they seemed tiny against the rugged backdrop of highland and glen. A stark 'V' cut the almost flat-calm surface of the loch as the sun began to peep slowly over the hills to the east and wisps of broken mist hung low over the shallows, the sun shafting through them, producing weird and ever-changing shapes.

It seemed that the dawn had heralded another pleasant day but after a short while the wind freshened from the north-west and a swell began to build, slowing the progress of the two boats.

In less than half an hour the front had moved directly overhead and the swell increased until it was over three feet. White horses raced along its crests, an awe-inspiring sight to four anglers more familiar with the calmer, shallower waters of the Norfolk Broads. Dark storm clouds raced down the valley, blotting out the hills on either side, and driving rain, almost horizontal, thrashed the surface to a foam as the boats rocked and dipped on the swell.

The small Seagull engine on the leading boat struggled to make headway against the increasing swell as it towed the other directly into the force of the wind. As both boats rode on the crests of waves their occupants stared down on to a turbulent sea of grey and white. As, inevitably, they dipped into the swell, each boat's view was cut off from the other by another huge white-topped wave. From the following boat, all that remained to remind them was a taut tow-rope disappearing abruptly into a sloping grey-green wall of water ahead.

Someone shouted to turn back and run with the wind, so slow and so nerve-racking was their progress. But the others knew what folly this would be. The direct course into the swell must be maintained. If it was deviated from, the boats could easily be capsized; their occupants, without life-jackets, would stand little chance in heavy clothing, over deep water and a great distance from the nearest shoreline.

Larger waters are always at the mercy of the elements. Stephen Harper keeps a wary eye on the gathering storm clouds.

They continued to steer their course into the teeth of the gale although water began to fill the boat wells, but slowly the distant shorelines changed as the two boats very gradually made headway. The power of the wind finally decreased as the boats entered the lee of a large protective island, finally to rest close to a rocky shoreline. Here four very wet and tired but relieved anglers could bail out their boats, take stock of the situation and even relax for a while as they watched the wind funnel through on either side.

Eventually the wind dropped slightly but still remained quite formidable. After fishing half-heartedly in sheltered bays out of the main force of the wind, the small group made a cautious return to camp, following the shoreline, with wary eyes watching the skies for any further deterioration in such a dangerously changeable climate.

A lesson had been learnt. Here the elements do not forgive easily and are not to be trifled with on this, an inland sea. Conditions such as these are probably some of the worst that

British anglers are likely to encounter. Weather is the first factor to be considered where safety is concerned, and if very bad weather is forecast, do not even consider venturing out on large waters. These conditions can sometimes develop so quickly that they can catch the angler unawares, so he must always be well equipped and preferably experienced for such occasions. On Scottish lochs, Irish loughs or English reservoirs, always use a reliable motor with plenty of reserve fuel and wear a life-jacket in all conditions. They are an inconvenience, often bulky and uncomfortable, but new designs now becoming available are slimmer and more wearable. After all, it's a small price to pay for your peace of mind and possibly your life.

The other aspects of safety in boats are mostly common sense. Most people come to grief either getting into or getting out of a boat and special care is needed as you load and unload, especially if there has been an overnight frost and the boat is covered in a thin sheet of ice. Fibreglass boats are especially unstable without the ballast of tackle, bags and another angler.

Some small boats, such as *an* 8-foot fibreglass dinghy, are only suited to one angler. If it is overloaded with two anglers and their gear, then disaster will surely follow. I have seen such a boat, with two anglers, almost swamped by the wash of a large cruiser on the River Bure at Wroxham. It was hilariously funny at the time but the incident could have had a much more serious outcome if the bank had not been so close.

The main insurance against such disasters is to know your boat and its limitations, familiarise yourself with the waters you fish, especially any dangerous areas such as rocky outcrops, be prepared for *any* eventualities and *always* have a healthy respect for the weather and what it can throw at the unprepared boat angler.

TEAMWORK

The most productive and efficient way to fish from a boat is alone. Disturbance is halved at a stroke and the catch rate can, in theory, be doubled. There are only so many fish within casting range and to have complete freedom of each and any swim can only mean more fish for the individual.

There is a certain magic about being alone in a boat at dawn but as the day wears on, as with many angling situations, there is no substitute for the companionship of an experienced and like-minded friend to share with you the triumphs and disasters of the day. Teamwork between two anglers in the confined space of a small boat seems to evolve over many sessions without any real conscious effort to develop it. Finally it becomes a natural and automatic process of co-ordination between both partners. They

Visitors are welcome but not when they want to eat what you have caught!

will instinctively know when their expertise is needed for the numerous tasks during the day's fishing, such as raising an anchor in an emergency or reeling in a second rod if a hooked fish becomes a problem. Many of these difficult situations can be avoided with the application of good teamwork.

WEIGHING FISH

Weighing fish in a boat is a simple matter with the smaller species and really no different from the same operation performed on the bank. But when a large fish is boated, pike in particular, it's a different story altogether – especially if there is any sort of swell to the water, inducing the boat to sway and rock.

A very large pike is perhaps best weighed and photographed on the bank, but this can often cost you and your companion lost sport if you have been lucky enough to hit a concentration of feeding pike. They won't feed for ever. Better to weigh the fish, take a couple of quick photographs, slip the fish back and carry on to catch maybe more and even larger fish. And there is one way to weigh a very large pike easily and accurately, even in a rocking boat.

I first devised the method whilst carp fishing. It was often difficult to get a clear reading on the Avon scales with fish over fifteen pounds, the needle doing its customary impersonation of Shakin' Stevens! I disconnected the landing-net handle and used it to steady the scales, forming a triangle between the handle and myself. In this way a much steadier and legible reading could be obtained very easily.

After using this method on the bank for carp, I soon realised that it had an ideal application in boat fishing, and I adapted it

with the use of an oar instead of the landing-net pole. Now, even in a strong wind, a legible and accurate reading can be obtained from a heavy fish without having to up-anchor and head for the bank with all the related disadvantages of a disturbed swim, loss of fishing time and further sport.

PHOTOGRAPHY

The secret of photography in boats is organisation and wide-angle lenses.

Cameras should be prepared, apertures set and shots practised well before the subject is ever brought on board. A fish, whatever its size, should not be allowed to thrash about in the well of the boat whilst cameras are made ready. Keep low in the boat by either sitting or kneeling. Avoid standing at all costs as it means that the fish has further to fall should it thrash and escape your grip. It is also safer for you.

Wide-angle and zoom lenses are a terrific help with on-board photography. There is no longer any need for the photographer to perch precariously in the bows as the captor leans dangerously backwards in the stern with his prize, trying to ensure that his head is not cut out of the picture.

Unless a photograph is to be taken, the fish should be returned to the water in the weigh sling and allowed to swim out of it. Often the movement towards the water after photography will reawaken a fish and a lively thrash can coincide with the fish being passed over the gunwhale. Inevitably the fish is dropped, bouncing on the gunwhale and either falling back into the boat or into the water. Either way the experience is *not* beneficial to the fish.

Necessities, Accessories and Luxuries

This section is devoted to the description and uses of some of the many and varied items related to boats and boat fishing. Some of these items you cannot possibly go boat fishing without, some merely aid efficiency and others are purely luxuries to add to comfort and enjoyment during the sometimes long hours spent afloat.

POLES

On many shallower waters throughout the country, and in particular on the Broads, poles are favoured rather than anchors for positioning a boat. (Oars can also be used on very shallow waters.) Some clubs, such as the Norwich and District Angling Association, have even banned the use of mud weights in their boats. The main reason for this has been the amount of mud left by untidy fishermen who have not cleaned the anchors before bringing them on board again.

Poles should be as straight as possible – neither so thick and heavy as to be ungainly nor so thin that they will break easily. Scaffold poles are used on some waters. If a pole is too long, it will impede striking; if it is too short, you will find yourself tying up with hands underwater – no fun on a freezing cold day in January with the wind pushing the water into your sleeves. Poles are unwieldy to push into the mud and can go in an incredible distance. A 15-foot pole is of little use in 10 feet of water and 5 feet of silt.

Their one major plus factor is that, once positioned, the boat is very stable, without the swinging motion encountered when using anchors. Four poles can be used for extra stability when legering for tench or bream. The extra two poles are tied to the rowlocks and provide a wonderfully stable platform to fish from, but these two extra underwater hazards almost outweigh their usefulness when boating a lively specimen.

Poles do have a tendency to pull out easily in strong winds, break completely, or somehow become untied if a secure knot hasn't been used. And getting poles out of the bottom can often be even harder than putting them in! Dotted throughout the broads are isolated, lonely poles, abandoned in the mud for ever, found to be irretrievable by some tired and boat-weary angler.

To align a boat side-on to the wind with poles without assistance is an art form in itself. To get one pole in, tie it, allow for the swing round and be ready with the second is not easy in a strong wind. It can be achieved so much more easily with two people.

Moving swims can also prove difficult. The poles laid along the boat impede rowing and it is best to tuck the tip of each pole under the main central seat, leaving the business end ready to be returned into the mud at each end of the boat.

On reflection, there seem to be many disadvantages and few real advantages in using poles and if at all possible I think I would rather use ties or anchors.

PETROL OUTBOARD   ANCHOR PULLEY   BATTERY FOR ELECTRIC OUTBOARD (BEHIND MAIN ENGINE)   MAIN UNHOOKING AREA KEPT FREE. PETROL CAN + SMALL ITEMS STASHED UNDER SEAT.   FISHFINDER   LARGE CUSHION BACK REST   IN COLLAPSABLE SCALES ETC.   CAMERAS, TACKLE   OUTRIGGERS   LIVE BAIT OR GROUND BAIT   ANCHOR CABLE SECURED IN CLEAT   ANCHORS ALWAYS OUTSIDE BOAT.

The author's boat layout for a one-man 9-foot fishing dinghy.

TIES

One method long used by Broadland anglers to secure their boats along a reed-fringed river or in the margins of a broad, with its many reed islands and outcrops, has proved to be very simple but very effective. The boat is tied to the reeds with two extra lengths of fine rope at bow and stern – very stable and secure and without the problems of anchor cables or poles for uncooperative fish to tangle with! It is the method I use whenever possible as the most stable, safe and easy way to secure a boat without any of the hassle associated with other methods. The bonus of being close to the reeds also means that the boat can be relieved of large items such as oars and landing nets.

Recently, instead of tying to the reeds, I have added large crocodile clips from a set of old jump leads to the ends of the ties – just another small detail that saves time and trouble in a day's fishing.

Another method akin to tying up to reeds is to use anchors on the bank. This method is used extensively on the tidal rivers of Broadland. Its effect is very much the same, giving very stable mooring without the usual disadvantages of using anchors.

ANCHORS AND ANCHORING

Three main types of anchor are used in British fresh water – the metal weight, usually 28 pounds; the concrete mud weight, with or without spikes; and the anchor hook and chain popular with trout anglers.

Three types of anchor used in British freshwater: the metal weight, the concrete mud weight and the spiked mud weight.

The metal 'weight' is a very reliable anchor which requires a thick rope and is prone to go deep into soft mud. With one of these at each end it takes a very strong wind to move a boat from its anchorage.

The concrete mud weight can easily be made using a plastic bucket as a mould, with a wire loop set into the top to take the anchor cable. Old paint cans can be used but do tend to rust and become dangerous. The introduction of two metal rods at right angles, forming four spikes, greatly increases the grip of the anchor, and also means that a much lighter weight can be used. Their effectiveness is improved on a longer rope which tips the anchor into its 'grip' position and increases its effectiveness.

The metal hook anchor is more often seen on trout reservoirs and sometimes incorporates a weak link for those nasty situations when the anchor becomes lodged in some underwater obstacle. The weak link breaks with increased pressure from above and

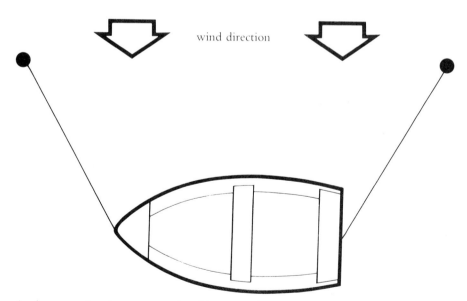

wind direction

Anchors are placed apart to angle cables towards boat, thereby reducing boat movement.

Fig 3   Anchoring in calm to moderate wind.

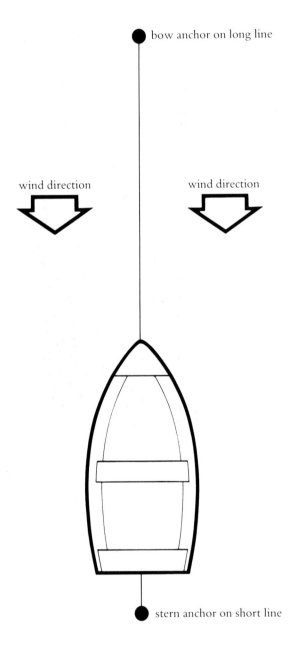

bow anchor on long line

wind direction   wind direction

stern anchor on short line

Fig 4 Anchoring in strong wind.

reverses the angle of pull on the anchor, which can usually be freed from the bottom. A length of chain immediately above the anchor helps to keep it in position by reducing

the strain exerted on the rope by the boat swinging in a strong wind. These anchors, however, are not as efficient as mud weights.

Other objects used as anchors are legion, but not recommended. I have seen large rocks, parts of car engines, metal trolley wheels, even buckets full of water. Neville Fickling swears by bricks with holes in. He probably swears at them too!

To fish from a boat, two anchors are essential. In normal situations – anything up to a moderate wind – most anglers prefer to position the boat side on. In this way both anglers can fish downwind and upwind. The two anchors should be lowered with as much distance as possible between them, the anchor cables forming a wide angle. This will minimise the swinging action characteristic when anchors are lowered too close together on very short lines.

In a strong wind, the boat should be positioned with its bow into the wind, the front anchor on a long line and the stern anchor on a very short line. This will help the boat to hold position and again reduce movement.

When a fish is hooked, especially one of the larger species, some anglers automatically pull up one anchor to reduce possible snagging problems by half. I have no doubt about the advantages of doing this but even with pike I have not found it really necessary. As long as the fish is not brought in too close before it is fully played out and a careful eye is kept on its direciton, the problem does not often arise. I cannot remember losing a fish in this way although I have had several fish swim round the anchor cable or pole. Luckily, I have always managed to free them successfully. The disturbance to the mud, a boat out of position plus anchors clanging about unnecessarily can all put a damper on sport and are therefore reasons enough why this precaution can sometimes be more of a hindrance than a help.

A cleat used to secure finer anchor cable.

Anchor Cables, Pulleys and Cleats

For the heavier anchors of the metal weight type, a thick sturdy cable of about 10-millimetre diameter is required. Anything finer on such a heavy anchor will cut into your hands on the retrieve, especially if the anchor has achieved a firm footing in the silt.

On lighter anchors, such as the concrete grip anchor, a thinner cable of about 5-millimetre diameter can be used. Whatever thickness you choose, it is best bought from a chandler's. They will usually stock the almost tangle-free braided nylon cable in a variety of thicknesses and strengths. Fifty feet will be ample for any swim encountered.

With the finer cable, pulleys can be employed, and the anchors can even be left outside the boat when in motion if the cable is secured in a cleat. Three types of cleat are commonly used, all available from chandlers.

Two types of cleat, used to secure thicker anchor cable.

The main use of the cleat, though, is once the anchor has been lowered. Whatever the depth of swim, the cable can be easily and conveniently secured without the hassle of having to tie knots each time the boat is moved.

OARS AND ROWLOCKS

Oars must be the correct length for the boat. I have often encountered oars too short for the boat, with which it is impossible to achieve much leverage. Much surface disturbance is caused in the process, the boat moving painfully slowly against a head wind.

When not in use, oars should be stashed

Anchors and mud do not need to be brought into the boat. Here, a concrete grip anchor is secured with ring and cleat.

Oar with retaining collar.

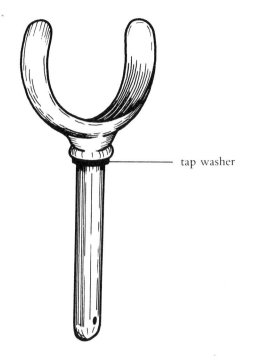

tap washer

Fig 5 Rowlock showing position of tap washer which helps to reduce noise.

away tidily together or even tied and hung over the side of the boat.

Some oars have collars which, to some degree, stop them slipping through the rowlocks. To be safer still, they can be tied to the rowlocks or, ideally, have special rowlocks fitted which remain attached with a bar through the oar.

Rowlocks must always be secured to the boat, because if they can fall out they will. And they should always be as silent as possible. A tap washer is useful here, pushed over the rowlock before it is slid into its retaining hole. This will cut out much of the usual noise and vibration. Thole-pins are even better than rowlocks and can be almost noiseless, but they are rarely seen on boats nowadays which is a great pity.

ENGINES

On the larger waters, such as lochs or broads, an engine is a necessity rather than a luxury.

The Shakespeare electric outboard with heavy duty, rechargeable battery.

No engine is totally reliable but some makes seem preferable to others. Johnson and Yamaha I have always found to be very good, the latter in the smaller models being especially light but powerful. Engines for fishing dinghies range from 2 to 6hp. In the United States that would class as a trolling motor, 35hp being more like the standard boat motor to get you to the swim.

A spare plug and tool kit are useful whenever afloat, as is a fuel funnel with built-in filter, which can save you hours cleaning out those carburettor jets. A spare shear-pin and split pin and a pair of pliers can spare you a long row, if not worse.

Chris Turnbull at the controls of the electric outboard. These engines are remarkably silent and very powerful.

As with boats, a good engine can be obtained second-hand. There is very little that can go wrong with them, being very simple machines. Some of the latest models now have tick-over and reverse gears, which can be very useful in a sticky situation.

On some waters – especially water reservoirs such as the Trinity group of broads, Ormesby, Filby, Rollesby and Lily – petrol engines are banned, except for rescue craft. This is where electric motors really come into their own. Very quiet, lightweight, pollution-free and surprisingly powerful, they are becoming more and more popular with anglers, even on waters where petrol engines are allowed, mainly because they are so quiet. Their only drawback is the range restricted by the limited power of a 12-volt battery. At about £200-plus they are not a cheap investment, but for many waters and situations, such as approaching a swim and trolling, they are ideal.

UNDERLAY AND CARPETING

When I first started pike fishing on the broads in the early 1970s, the common practice amongst anglers was to take several sacks and lay them on the deck to protect the pike from serious damage. As time passed, more and more people began to use foam carpet underlay or carpet itself, sometimes cut exactly to fit the shape of the deck. Now in Norfolk it is rare to see a boat not equipped with some form of padding and it should be used for all species. Some novices and 'part-time' anglers still need to be educated.

I personally prefer foam underlay or the foam side of foam-backed carpet to receive the fish. Carpet itself, if not very wet, can take a lot of slime from a fish and possibly do as much harm as good, acting as one gigantic brush. Underlay does have other advantages besides the protection of the fish.

Wall-to-wall carpeting. Its main function is to protect the fish but it also helps to keep noise and vibration down.

The main one is that it helps to keep down noise and vibration from the boat and its occupants. Other advantages include a non-slip surface, handy in some fibreglass boats especially in wet weather, and slightly warmer feet in the depths of winter!

ROD RESTS

When legering for tench or bream, long rod rests used outside the boat are a great help. Normal rod rests can be used with buzzer bars and simply taped to two garden canes or metal tubes and pushed into the mud. Total stability is achieved, the rods and their bite indicators now completely free from the inevitable boat movements of even the quietest and most careful angler.

Other boat rod rests as shown in the photographs include a simple clip-on rod-rest head, a multiple rest using a Drennan swingtip rod rest, and the screw-on outriggers used mainly when trolling for predatory fish. An advantage of these outriggers is that the rods are completely out of the boat and not across the gunwales, giving the boat angler much more room and freedom to move about.

One last method, which is not really a rod rest in the true sense, is the use of lengths of fan belt pinned along the gunwales ridged side up. This forms innumerable 'rod rests' all along the boat wherever a rod is laid, with the line still free to run should a take occur. It also reduces the noisy bang and clatter of rods on the gunwale that can sometimes occur if the boat rocks or a rod is

rods mounted on buzzer
bars fore and aft so only
2 rests are needed for 2 rods

The angler should face toward
the intended swim, the boat
stabilised with 2 or even
4 poles. Rods should be
positioned outside the
boat on extra-long
rod rests pushed
into the bottom.

'A' indicates normal
bow and stern
positioning
of poles.

'B' indicates
positioning
of 2 other poles tied to
rowlocks for extra
stability.

Fig 6   Legering afloat.

A simple clip-on rod rest, useful for float fishing.

A multiple rest made from a Drennan swingtip rod rest.

A screw-on outrigger used for trolling or float trolling. These keep rods out of the boat and give the angler more space.

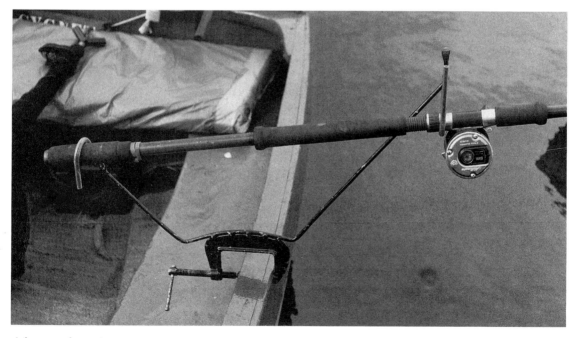

A home-made outrigger.

inadvertently knocked. Especially useful in an emergency, a rod or rods can be very quickly moved in a crisis without having to be taken from rests or outriggers. It is also a very cheap solution to an ever-present problem for boat anglers.

DROGUES AND DRIFT CONTROL

Trout anglers are the masters of drogue fishing but it does have its uses in fishing for the other freshwater species, especially when using artificial lures or trolling baits on the oars for the predatory species.

A drogue is a small underwater parachute. It can be easily made with a 4-foot square of nylon or canvas with a small hole at its centre. Cords 3 feet long are attached at each corner and linked by a swivel to a 4-foot length of cord which is tied to the stern, bows or a rowlock, depending on the force of the wind and the required speed of the boat. A drogue will slow the boat's movement considerably, allowing the water to be covered slowly and thoroughly, and many more fish to be covered.

A limitation when fishing on the drogue is that the boat obviously moves in a straight line only, directly downwind. In lighter winds, the drogue can be replaced by a drift control rudder fitted to the stern. This allows the boat to be steered across and downwind to cover headlands and contour lines.

CLOTHING

Clothing is one of the most important factors and should be considered very carefully by any would-be boat angler. On the bank the wind may seem moderate, the rain light and the temperatures bearable. Out on the water, exposed to anything that the weather can throw at you, it is a different situation entirely. 'Two coats warmer on the bank' is an oft-quoted phrase in Norfolk and not that far from the truth.

Modern thermal underwear is light, very warm and does not restrict movement. There is no longer any excuse for looking like the Michelin man! Outer garments must be waterproof and windproof. Waxed cotton fits the bill ideally.

Waxed cotton one-piece suits are now very popular for winter fishing but I personally still prefer the freedom of separate

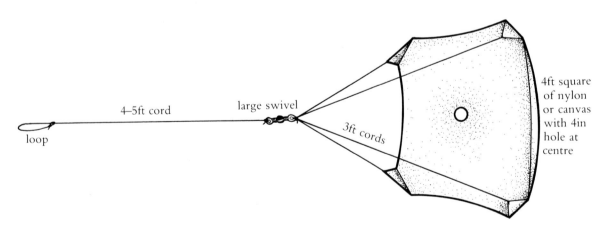

Fig 7   The drogue.

Wrapped up well against the weather, Kevin Maxfield heads out to another swim.

leggings and jacket, especially during the spring and autumn months, when it can be very cold and very warm all in a morning.

Since much heat is lost from the head, hats are essential. The best are woollen. Better still are balaclavas for those really cold winds, all tucked inside a roomy waterproof hood. But don't forget the sunny days. They do happen occasionally and sunshades in the form of baseball-type hats are becoming increasingly popular, especially with lure anglers.

Cold feet in winter can ruin a day's enjoyment. In a boat there is not much you can do about the problem. Stamping your feet or keeping on the move, as you would on the bank, is obviously out. In the old days I would take an old blanket to wrap round my feet but with the advent of 'moon boots' the problem no longer arises. These are the answer to cold feet and for anyone who has 'managed' with ordinary boots they cannot be recommended highly enough. Since using them I cannot remember suffering from cold feet, even on days when we have had to smash the ice to fish – a real asset for the winter boat angler. To keep the hands warm and dry, spare gloves and a towel, kept close by, are the answer.

While on the subject of keeping warm, there is no substitute for hot food, soup and drinks. They can help stave off the winter blues much better than cold sandwiches and cans of beer. There's nothing better than hot bacon and eggs washed down with a fresh mug of tea all cooked on a small stove set in a windproof container in the well of the boat. And to enjoy a perfect cup of tea every time from a flask, fill it with hot water only (sugar if required), and take tea-bags and milk separately – a perfect cuppa every time!

SEATING

A cushion of some sort is almost indispensable for a day afloat. Some anglers use a small inflated innertube. I have always used a large slab of foam in a sealed waterproof bag, large enough to lie on in the well of the boat if wind and weather become ferocious. Collapsible chairs can be used, but only safely during mild weather, and then in flat-bottomed boats such as punts. A collapsible back rest, fixed to a seat, is a much better proposition.

THE BAILER

Never go afloat without a bailer. There are innumerable tasks to which this very simple item can be put, bailing out the boat being only one of the more obvious. It can also help greatly in answering a call of nature in safety, instead of perching precariously over the side of a rocking, swaying boat. For this reason it has gained many names less formal than its usual one!

CUDDIES AND CANOPIES

The wind lashes the rain against your back and the water runs down onto the seat. Rain drips from the hood into your face and hands are soon cold and wet. Even in waxed cottons it is uncomfortable and everything seems such a great effort. The tea is cold almost before it hits the cup and the sandwiches are soon soggy.

These are the worst conditions to befall the boat angler. A combination of rain and strong winds, especially in winter, is in no way an enjoyable situation. Oh for a cuddy or a canopy to protect against the wind and rain! A retreat between casts and a haven from the weather where a hot drink can be brewed in comfort.

Fishing umbrellas, saviour of the bank angler and supporter of the bivvy, are of little use in a boat. They can be used against rain in calm conditions but are more trouble than their worth in even the slightest of winds, unless you are totally organised (*see* Punt Fishing for Bream, page 66). Much better is a pram-type canvas canopy which can be erected in bad weather, or, better still, a fibreglass boat with a cuddy over the bows, and the fishing carried out towards the stern area of the boat. With a craft such as this, you can even consider overnight stays on the water, a great asset when fishing lochs or loughs miles from base camp.

DEPTH FINDING

Whenever anglers think of boats their thoughts immediately turn to catching fish, but boats can help dramatically towards the capture of fish even with no rods aboard. I am, of course, referring to depth finding, an exercise often carried out in the close season on waters where boats are sometimes not allowed during the season. Much can be learned of a water, in great detail – not only its depths but the nature of the bottom, weed beds, snags, and even observation of fish not clearly visible from the bank.

In its simplest form, on shallow waters such as the broads a rod can be used to gauge the depth along the rod rings and to test whether the bottom is hard gravel or soft mud. The next simple step is to make a plumb-line using an old reel that can be clamped to the side of the boat. Non-stretch line, such as dacron, is used with a heavy lead or even a bottom sampler attached at the end. Tiny plastic tags are tied securely into the line at one- or two-foot intervals with measurements written on in indelible ink – a simple and cheap but time-consuming method of depth finding, still vastly superior to rod and plumb-line from the bank.

A boat for the lochs and loughs?

The real answer to the problem is an electronic echo-sounder – at around £50 not a cheap item of tackle but one that will pay for itself over and over in knowledge and fish as the years pass by. It will also tell you much more about a water than its depth. For instance, a thin, sharply defined reading will tell you that the bottom is hard. A wider, less well-defined band shows a softer, muddy bottom, and even weed beds show up in a similar indistinct fashion , registering at the depths they occur. In fact, the more an echo-sounder is used and experience gained, the more detail will be revealed and information accumulated on the many charts and drawings that will become an indispensable aid to fish finding.

FISH FINDERS

And talking of fish finding, that of course can now be performed electronically too!

Much has been said and written about the ethics of using fish finders, but make no mistake, they are definitely here to stay, their popularity increasing steadily within the angling world. Some anglers believe that their use is unethical and that they take out of angling all the skill of watercraft and the enjoyment of reading a water to find the fish. Similar negative comments were made about the electronic bite alarm in the 1950s, and look where that is today!

It is a fact that fish finders work. They will locate your quarry and tell you a great deal about the nature of bottom contours, snags and weed beds. To watch that large shape or shapes approaching the area you know your bait to be in is fantastically exciting, but the fish still has to be tempted and

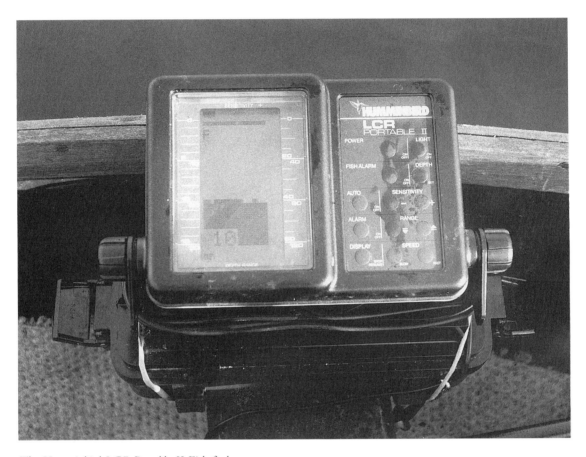

The Humminbird LCR Portable II Fish finder.

caught! A fish finder will not do that for you or make you a better angler but it will even the odds on a very large water such as a loch, lough or reservoir, where a bait cast from a rod is literally a drop in the ocean.

Originally developed for marine fishermen and therefore very deep water, some models are of limited use in very shallow water. Marine models operate best at depths between 120 and 300 feet although the depth scales sometimes show 2,500 feet! (Loch Morar is the deepest freshwater lake in Britain at 1,017 feet.) An electronic signal is sent through the water from the transducer of the echo-sounder. This then bounces back from the bed of the lake and other objects or fish in the vicinity, and the information is decoded and transferred either to a paper read-out or to a small screen of tiny squares called pixels that make up a composite picture of the underwater scene. Several makes are now available, the most popular being Lowrance, Fuji and Humminbird. The Humminbird is the model I am most familiar with. Prices range from about £200 to well over £1,000, and some tackle shops now hire them out for about £10 per day. The more expensive the model, the more extras there will be and the more detailed the read-out. The top of the range Humminbird, for example, retailing at about £400, indicates the fish in red and all other objects in black (in the lower-range models, everything is shown in black). The air in the swim bladders of the fish distinguish them from inanimate objects such as weed, snags or irregular bottom contours.

For some boat anglers a fish finder will never be a necessity, the waters fished being either too small or too shallow to warrant its use. The price is still prohibitive to many pockets. But, for the dedicated boat angler of the larger and deeper of Britain's freshwater lakes and rivers, I predict that a fish finder will become an indispensable item of equipment in future seasons, directly responsible for the location of many very large fish of a variety of species.

PART 2

The Big River Approach

by Bill Rushmer

Bill Rushmer has for many years specialised in fishing for the wide variety of species found in the tidal River Thames. Whether the species is dace or roach, perch or bream, carp or pike, Bill's enthusiasm and knowledge are extensive.

His fish are usually caught from the punts of the famous Francis Francis Angling Club, the last traditional punt club in the world. The rules, methods, procedures and history of this remarkable club make for fascinating reading and give an insight into how angling was practised in years long past on our greatest of tidal rivers.

When not punt fishing on the Thames, Bill spends his time as head of science at a London school and organising one of the largest and most active sections of the National Association of Specialist Anglers – the London region. This includes much work for charity and teaching younger anglers the correct way to approach our sport.

SH

I belong to a very special club, the Francis Francis Angling Club. This club, named after the famous Thames angler of the 1800s, is thought to be the last traditional punt club left in the world, and in this chapter I hope to pass on some of the knowledge of the big river approach gained by club members.

The club is based at Twickenham on the tidal Thames. Its headquarters is the Barmy Arms at Twickenham Embankment, conveniently within 100 yards of where the club's punts are moored on the tidal Thames.

The club specialises in fishing the Thames in some of its widest coarse fishing areas. This venue is also potentially one of the most dangerous, with a high volume of boat traffic in summer tides, and – worst of all – savage winter floods. These are not conditions for the novice or the faint-hearted. Nevertheless, the venue can be mastered to provide some excellent sport.

The club's punts are all fairly large, robust and of various traditional designs. They are of very heavy timber construction with knees and treads of oak. All punts have wet wells fitted as standard to retain the catch. These lie about a third of the way down the length of the punt and comprise a section sealed off by heavy timber bulkheads with water entering and leaving through grills fitted in the sides and bottom. Fish can be retained safely in the well before being transported to the embankment for weighing in. The fish always arrive in first-class condition – far better than if kept in keepnets. Fish dragged along behind a boat in keepnets suffer untold damage that would never be tolerated in the Francis Francis Angling Club.

Every punt has its own gear stored in a nearby yard and taken aboard on every outing. The gear consists of a paddle, a pushing pole and two heavyweight rye-peck mooring poles. These rye-peck poles are made from heavy pine of up to 6 inches diameter. They are over 20 feet long and are

Puntsmen Len Broadley and Tony Myott fishing amongst the boats of the tidal Thames.
Photo: Bill Rushmer

fitted with heavy metal spikes. They are used to moor the punt across the swim. The spikes of the poles are worked into the river bed to give a firm positive hold at each end of the punt.

The great advantage of rye-peck poles over anchor weights is that the punt is held firmly in place yet allowed to rise and fall with the tide. This allows club members to fish in comfort from punts held firmly across the stream. An added bonus is that by means of two quick-release knots the punt can be broken free of its moorings very quickly to leave the rye-pecks in position. This action is often needed with the army of blind Sunday sailors who inhabit the lower Thames in summer.

Unfortunately, two punts have been hit when moored across the stream, but I am pleased to report that in neither case was the punt sunk. A rowing eight with a short-sighted cox went into the side of a moored punt in shallow water. The eight folded in two and sank. Its bows were embedded in the side of the punt and were cut off flush, and the very point of the eight is still stuck in the side of Dave Stevens' punt. A similar fate was suffered by a one-man sculling boat. Yes, our punts are heavy and strong, as are our puntsmen. They have to carry on their shoulders the punt's gear of two rye-pecks, pushing pole and paddle lashed together from the yard to the punt every time they go out. It has been estimated that this gear can weigh over 140 pounds.

Although membership of the Francis Francis is open to all, prospective new members are expected to attend several

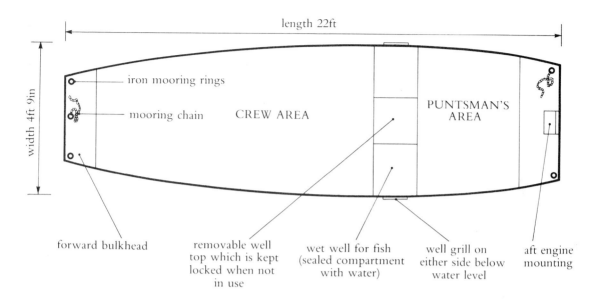

Fig 8   The Francis Francis punt.

Sunday-morning matches as guests before they can be put forward for membership. Many apply to the club expecting to be able to take a punt out for fishing whenever they want. However, for safety reasons this privilege is not available to ordinary members but is reserved for those with proven boat-handling ability. These members are the puntsmen. To become a puntsman the ordinary member must elect to become a trainee puntsman for a year. During this time, the trainee puntsman will be the re-sponsibility of a senior puntsman, who will teach him watercraft, poling and mooring techniques. After the year comes the punting test, under the strict supervision of another senior puntsman. The trainee will be expec-ted to demonstrate that he can handle the punt with a pushing pole in the fast waters of the tideway and moor the punt safely in confined spaces using rye-pecks. This may appear to be rather strict, but the safety of the crew is in the hands of the puntsman.

Most puntsmen are allocated to a punt and are responsible for the maintenance and

care of that punt. My punt is the only duck punt in the club. With a length of about 16 feet and a maximum width of 4 feet 10 inches, it is also the smallest punt in the club. As a duck punt, it is our only pointed punt – in the past it had to be pushed through the reeds to get in range of ducks. A large cannon was fitted to the punt. This took a charge of nearly 1½ pounds of gunpowder. As the cannon was fixed, the punt was aimed at any ducks and the cannon then fired. Being small, this punt gives me the advantage of being able to moor in confined spaces which will not accommodate our larger punts. This is very important when fishing between moored houseboats in winter floods and is a technique that has given me some excellent results in club matches.

As the punt is moored across the stream for fishing, the angler can allow the current to pull the float away from the punt. Under these conditions the centrepin reel is the most effective tool. All club members use centrepins, with a 4½-inch Stanton the most popular choice. I prefer to use a similar reel

Two large punts of the 'Francis Francis' Angling Club

Photo: Bill Rushmer

manufactured by a local engineering works. This reel is handleless, wide-drummed, light-running on ball bearings and has a diameter of 4½ inches. The reel is fitted with an adjustable pressure plate which acts as a drag – very useful for playing carp. I have only seen this reel for sale in the local Hounslow Angling Centre. The reel is loaded with no more than 100 yards of line to avoid bedding problems and is also loaded so that the line leaves the top of the reel. This allows for better float control with fewer tangles caused by side winds.

Generally, club members use shorter rods than bank anglers because bites often come very close to the punt, even directly under the rod top. I use a home-made 11-foot stiff-actioned carbon rod for the majority of my trotting from the punt.

Although many club members use dacron line, as they believe it gives them better float control, I still prefer nylon lines. The strength of line is much higher than that used by bank anglers on the same venue since the

The punt is moored across the stream and the angler can allow the current to pull the float and tackle away.

Photo: Bill Rushmer

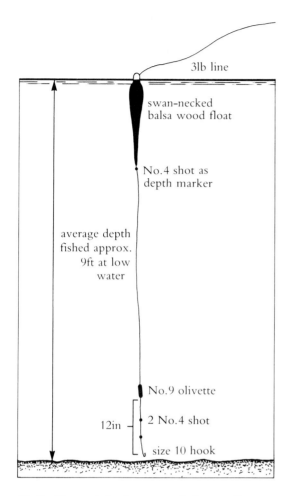

3lb line

swan-necked
balsa wood float

No.4 shot as
depth marker

average depth
fished approx.
9ft at low
water

No.9 olivette

12in 2 No.4 shot

size 10 hook

Fig 9 Float and shotting pattern for boat angling.

fish has to be pulled upstream to the moored punt. On most Sunday-morning matches I use 3-pound line tied directly to the hook.

Floats and shotting patterns are again more robust than those used by bank anglers. About 7BB swan-necked balsa is the most commonly used float, with a shotting pattern that concentrates the weight near the hook. This gets the bait down to the bottom of the often rather turbulent water. A non-toxic tungsten olivette is used in place of bulk shot. This gets the bait down quicker and

gives the added advantage of a more stream-lined terminal rig. The olivette is placed about 12 inches from the hook with two or three No. 4 shot spaced out between the hook and olivette. A No. 4 shot is placed directly under the float to act as a depth marker should the float slip (*see* Fig 9).

Bread is the most popular bait used in the club. The bread hookbait is prepared in the traditional Thames style – a style that appears to be lost to today's specimen world. The white crusts are cut off a loaf and soaked in water for about quarter of an hour. The wet bread is then left overnight compressed in sheets of newspaper to half-dry. This produces a dense soft white bait that is deadly to most tidal species, including carp.

The groundbait is prepared from stale white loaves which are left to soak in cold water rather than hot water. It is then mashed and kneaded to remove excess water. A little white breadcrumb is added to provide a stiff, dense, white groundbait that breaks up at the bottom of the swim where it is needed. Often the groundbait is placed in a bait dropper which is made from two salad shakers. This bait dropper is weighed down by a 1½-pound sea lead. The groundbait is placed in the cavity between the two salad shakers and lowered by a cord from the side of the punt to the bottom (*see* Fig 10). The dropper is worked occasionally by a pull on the cord to provide a continuous stream of groundbait through the swim.

CARP

Although I have caught carp from the banks of the tidal Thames, the punt gives me many advantages over the bank angler. I can fish virgin swims that are inaccessible to the bank angler and pre-bait with great accuracy without any fear of the dreaded swim jumpers. The true potential of tidal carp may never be known as the venue is so large

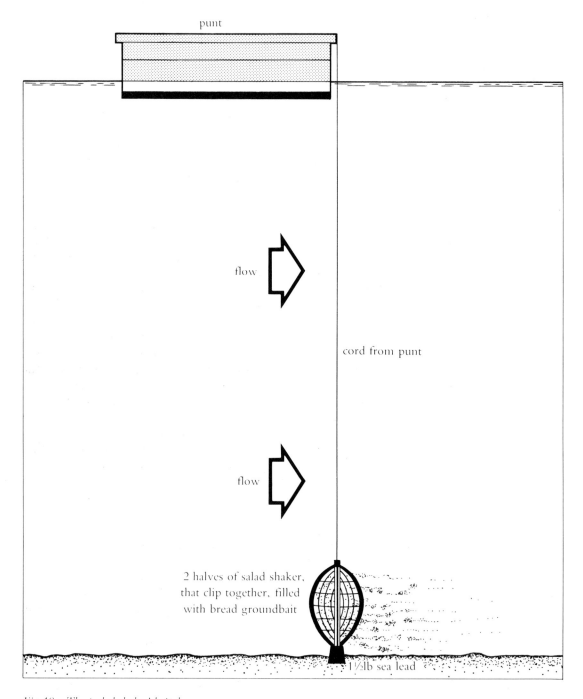

punt

flow

cord from punt

flow

2 halves of salad shaker,
that clip together, filled
with bread groundbait

1½lb sea lead

Fig 10 The 'salad shaker' bait dropper.

with many areas that are never fished. However, it is known that there are carp present to well over thirty pounds. It may be possible for a carp to spend its whole life in the tideway without ever seeing an angler's bait. Re-captures are rare and there are no carp with names. This is not the venue for second-hand carp, as so many of our popular fisheries have become. The records of the Francis Francis show that carp captures are increasing, as is the average size. The average carp caught on Sunday-morning matches is well into double figures, which is surprising when the time fished is taken into consideration – from approximately 8.30 a.m. to 12 noon.

In 1985 I was a trainee puntsman with David Stevens, a senior puntsman with great experience and a master at handling a punt under all conditions. David had already taught me summer punt tactics and the ways of the local weir. Now he was teaching me how to handle the low water of the annual run-off. During this period the half weir at Isleworth is taken out of use. This lowers the water at Twickenham by about five feet and allows repair work and inspection of the bridges, lock gates and boats in the section. The low water is a real test of navigation as there is the danger of running aground on the many shallow bars that are now very near the surface. Naturally, this affects the fishing as the shoals are now in a much more confined space.

In early October David and I were faced with a run-off with very poor fishing. Neither he nor I had had a bite. Other punts were suffering similarly, with only one chub being caught that morning. David decided on a move for the last 1½ hours to a swim near Teddington lock. He skilfully moored the punt just in front of a deep hole with 8 feet of water at its deepest.

'Under these conditions this swim produces the odd good carp,' said David.

We trotted for 1¼ hours without a bite.

'I'm going to lighten off for the last ten minutes to try to catch a dace or perch,' I told David.

'Go for it, Bill, but be careful. There are still carp in the swim' was David's reply. I trotted through with a single maggot on a size 18 hook to a 1.7-pound trace and was soon landing a sizeable perch that could have been worth second place when on the next trot I struck a violent bite. It was a good fish that I first thought was a large perch, but I quickly realised that it was too heavy to be a perch. A tench, I thought – but David disagreed.

'It's a carp without any doubt' was David's comment. Then he saw what I had seen.

'It's got no scales of any description, but I can't see that clearly. It must be a tench and it's a real monster,' David said.

Boat traffic was approaching and the danger of a cut line became a distinct possibility. Seeing the danger, David pulled the quick-release knots to free the punt from its rye-peck. Once the punt was free, David used it as a shield to protect my line from the boat traffic. Slowly the fish started to tire and David decided to beach the punt to land the fish. We were about 200 yards below where I originally hooked the fish. We could see the fish clearly – it was a perfect leather carp. Slowly the tired fish was brought to the landing net to be netted by David. I was delighted, as it was the first leather to be caught in one of our club matches.

That carp won the match and on checking with the scalesman I saw it was recorded as 'carp (bald), eleven pounds eight ounces'.

I said, 'It's a leather carp.'

'Not in this club. You'll have to take it up at the next meeting. Until then it's a bald carp' was the scalesman's reply.

That Tuesday at our meeting the club officially recognised my carp as a leather carp and I was firmly reminded that this was a punt club. If I ever landed a fish from the bank again I would be disqualified.

A double-figure common carp for Bill Rusher. Unlike stillwater carp, this fish had possibly never been captured before.

Photo: Bill Rushmer

At the end of the season I took my punting test under Len Broadley. Thanks to David's teaching I passed to become a qualified puntsman. I could now take a punt out at any time, which gave me the flexibility I wanted.

My first outing as a puntsman was on the first Saturday morning of the next season. My passenger was the club chairman, Tim Ward. We went to another swim by the lock but met with little success until I scaled down to hit another carp. Again the slip knots to the rye-peck were pulled and Tim used the punt as a shield from the boat traffic. It was virtually an action replay of the previous carp, but this was a common carp of ten pounds six ounces.

Boats are a problem on the tidal Thames and have been responsible for the loss of many carp. Perhaps the best carp to have been lost was a terrific specimen approaching thirty pounds which was lost by club presi-

dent Bill Goldstone when he was fishing from my punt. This fish was hooked on a huge lump of bread trotted down on heavy tackle. The fish gave a terrific bite and was being played with heavy sidestrain. It appeared to be tiring and everything was looking good. It was clearly seen several times as it came to the surface but then kited round to the side; the line must have touched a sharp area on the propellor of our static engine and was cut. It was bad luck, but it proved that bigger carp than we thought were present in that swim. Another carp caught by Len Broadley was the best fish of the day. It was a magnificent common of nearly fourteen pounds but it looked very small compared with Bill Goldstone's lost carp.

At the time of writing I am fishing for tidal carp using sweetcorn as bait with some rather mixed results. Heavy boat traffic and bad weather have been a problem but I feel that there is still great potential in this venue.

ROACH AND BREAM

Although dace are the predominant species caught by bank anglers, the punt angler tends to ignore dace to fish for roach and bream. In recent years the punt anglers have been concentrating their efforts on bream as they are producing such high bag weights.

Roach are a species which have been in decline on the tideway for more than ten years. No longer is it common to see bags of roach approaching sixty pounds with fish averaging three-quarters of a pound to be made in under four hours. The club's records show that the average best roach caught on a Sunday morning is now only seven and a half ounces compared with nearly one pound four ounces ten years ago.

Shoals of roach are still present, though much rarer. Last winter I took my small punt in by some houseboats to fish the narrow run between two rows of boats. The space was so narrow that I could not turn the punt to fish across the stream. Instead I moored alongside one houseboat to trot down the side of another boat, placing three large balls of groundbait loaded with stones at the top of the swim. I plumbed the depth at about 6 feet and started to trot a piece of wet bread through the swim on a size 12 hook. The float had not travelled more than six inches before it disappeared. A firm strike and I was into a ten-ounce roach. This was followed by six more roach in the next six casts. The roach continued to feed for the full length of the match, which I won with just over thirty-five pounds of roach. All the roach were over eight inches long as the club still fishes to the old Thames size limits. This has the advantage that we are still fishing to the same standards as in 1927, which means that records can be compared.

I made several catches of roach of over thirty pounds last year but they were all made in the winter on bread from selected swims. The size of the roach was below the old standards, with few fish over the one-pound mark. It was noticeable that all the fish appeared to be young and very healthy, which is a good sign for the future. I look forward to the day when I can make catches approaching sixty pounds with individual fish to nearly two pounds, as I used to do in the 1960s.

Whilst roach bags have declined, the bream catches are becoming remarkable, with individual bags of over 100 pounds being regularly recorded. These bream catches are normally made during October and November, when the bream shoal up. It is noticeable that when the tidal river produces its bream other selected areas of non-tidal Thames are also producing similar catches. The other year I had two good bags of 132 pounds and 147 pounds from swims near Teddington at low water. On both occasions

the fish were feeding from the first cast and continued until poor light or changing tide stopped fishing. These bream averaged between one and three-quarter and two pounds, with individual fish to over four pounds. Bread again appears to be the best bait, whilst maggots and worms also produce good sport. I believe that with the upsurge in the bream population, a bag of well over 200 pounds is possible.

PREDATORS

As the bream shoals have increased, so have the pike that feed on them. Some of the pike appear to be very well-proportioned fish, unlike the long thin dace-feeding pike that are so common on Thames weir sills. These better fish seem to be found near the bream hot spots.

In February 1987 I was lucky to have my half-term holiday during one of the few weeks that the river was not flooded. I arrived at my swim to set up with an 11-foot hollow-glass rod with a 2½-pound test curve, a Mitchell 300 reel loaded with 12-pound line, with terminal tackle consisting of a pilot float holding the equivalent of two swan shot leading to a wire trace holding two size 8 trebles to complete the outfit. A roach livebait was used, the float set at 7 feet and trotted away from the punt on an incoming tide. Almost immediately I had a run and struck into terrific resistance. After a while I realised that this was an exceptional fish as it had been fighting so hard for so long without leaving the bottom. Eventually after several long runs the fish tired and approached the surface. I could not believe my eyes as I netted the monster. I quickly unhooked the pike and placed it in the well with the lid firmly in place and headed back to Twickenham Embankment to have it properly weighed. At thirty-three pounds six ounces this pike is thought to be the River Thames record,

Bill Rushmer's massive 33lb 6oz pike, the River Thames record.
Photo: Bill Rushmer

but I still believe that there are even larger specimens in some of the more obscure swims of the tideway.

Perch is another species that is also improving in both quantity and quality. Last year the club match record for a perch went to two pounds three ounces, with many others around the two-pound mark being recorded, but this does not represent the true picture since both spinning and livebaiting are banned in club matches. Small livebaits appear to be the answer to the bigger perch. I know of a three-pound nine-ounce perch and several others approaching the three-pound mark that were caught on such baits. This year I am determined to spend more time using small livebaits in amongst the moored boats where I have seen large perch hunting. I will modify the grills on the well of my punt so that I can keep a supply of suitable baits for when I need them. It is possible that most of the slacker swims hold good perch in winter, as recent reports are showing this trend.

Perch are thriving in the tidal Thames. The largest of this bag weighed 2lb 1oz although 3 pounders are not unknown.

Photo: Bill Rushmer

HISTORY

The records of the Francis Francis provide the most accurate available history of fishing in the tidal Thames. Alwyne Wheeler of the Natural History Museum used these records in his book on the tidal Thames to compare the trends and cycles in the fish populations on this venue. He has been a great friend to the club and takes a great interest in the club's catches. He is always available to identify the more unusual fish that are sometimes caught. These include sea species, game fish and the odd fish that has escaped from a garden pond or from a fish tank.

These records are more than just a record of fishing catches over the years. They are a record of the spirit and determination of a group of local people. This becomes very obvious when one looks at the records of meetings held during the Second World War, when all who remained to fish the club's matches were in reserved occupations, such as watermen taking valuable supplies by barge from the Port of London to the power stations higher up the river.

In early 1940 the club's minutes show that the club sent £25 to the famous *Daily Mirror* columnist Cassandra to buy the troops, who were bogged down in trench warfare, darts and dart boards for when they were not fighting. In 1940 £25 was a lot of money and shows the generosity of the few club members who remained.

Air raids were a continual problem, with the Germans constantly trying to disrupt the flow of goods along the Thames. Often these raids would occur during a club match and there was the real danger of one of our punts being hit. This was discussed at a meeting where it was decided that the club would fish on regardless. Members had to put up with air raids during the week and they were determined not to give Mr Hitler the satisfaction of disrupting their fishing.

At a meeting in 1942 the members' wives complained that their husbands were taking all the bread to go fishing. Under this type of pressure the club members knew they were beaten, and bread was banned as bait. Members were forced to fish with worms instead!

During the Twickenham blitz the club was holding a meeting with roads less than 200 yards away on fire and continually bombed.

One member asked, 'Do we stop and go to the air-raid shelter?'

'Don't be silly. Sid has just got another round in,' came the reply.

Naturally, the meeting continued throughout the whole of the Twickenham blitz, in which a good proportion of the town was destroyed. But not the Francis Francis Angling Club. Their spirit and determination saw them through those troubled times.

The minutes also contain details of medals won by members, deaths of members, and when members were captured and released. But above all they are a record of the lives of a group of extraordinary anglers and punts-men.

THE FUTURE

The club will continue to fish from punts in the traditional style and hopefully build up its membership to full strength. There are already plans to build another punt out of traditional materials to a 1923 design. I cannot see, with the determination and keenness of members, that the club will ever fold.

The fishing, however, as in many parts of the country, is constantly changing. On the tideway the trend seems to be towards more carp and bream, with improved sport from predatory species.

Last year, the London region of the National Association of Specialist Anglers was very short of prizes for a raffle. I put forward a day's punt fishing as a prize. The winner, John Trevor-Jones, and Peter Garvan arrived for a day's punt fishing in November. We started off by trotting to catch a mixture of roach, dace and bream before changing to livebaiting, when we were almost immediately into fish. We ended up with fourteen pike, six perch to two pounds thirteen ounces and a zander of six pounds seven ounces. The perch was taken on a large dace livebait by John whilst I caught the zander. This zander may be another river record, but I am convinced that it will soon be bettered as the species spreads through the Thames system. I have taken another zander since that day. It was a small fish of one and a half pounds but it proves that the earlier fish was not a one-off.

Chub are also becoming more common and increasing in size. Last winter bank anglers were regularly adding chub to their bags of dace from Twickenham Embankment. We also had sixteen chub reported in a club match but unfortunately the majority were undersize.

I hope that in this chapter I have given the reader some insight into the world of the punt angler on a big river like the Thames. To do well it is important to spot trends. I am convinced that if there were similar clubs to the Francis Francis on other large rivers the members would enjoy similar success.

The Small River Approach

In total contrast to Bill Rushmer's experiences on the wide expanses of the very busy tidal Thames, my own experiences on the narrow upper rivers of Norfolk reveal some interesting comparisons.

The variance in size of these rivers dictates a wide difference in boat type and approach and, as Bill has explained, there is probably no river as busy, with all types of boat traffic, as the area of the River Thames that he fishes. On the narrow upper rivers, you can spend the whole day without seeing another craft, apart, perhaps, from another lone canoeist, on the river for a completely different reason. But, whatever the size of the waterway, the reason for boat fishing remains the same – easy access, which on the upper rivers can often pose many problems for the bank angler.

'No Fishing;' 'No Access for Anglers'; 'Private Land – Keep Off'. The negative aspect of these signs is only too familiar to most anglers, and as the seasons pass by the situation does not improve. Access is often the major problem in finding good fishing. But many of the more secluded waters, in particular the upper rivers, can be fished using a small boat or, better still, a canoe.

On the larger, tidal, waters, an ancient right of navigation exists which stems from the days of the Magna Carta. All boats are permitted by common law, as is angling. On non-tidal rivers the situation is more complicated and differs from river to river, and even from stretch to stretch. But if a right of navigation does exist on a particular stretch then the angler can launch a boat and fish from it provided he has a current fishing licence and observes the fishing rights. A quiet enquiry in the right direction, should it be needed, will often bring surprising results, proving of great benefit to the serious angler in search of seclusion and good fishing.

I first used a boat on the upper rivers of Norfolk during the close seasons. Many enjoyable hours were spent spotting fish in new and old areas, familiarising myself with swims not easily visible from the bank and searching out new and inaccessible lies for chub, roach and barbel. So much water can be covered from a boat in this way for so little effort. To drift with the current at dusk on a still evening, noting the swims where the roach prime, is an experience not to be missed. Baiting can also be carried out from a canoe, and overhanging branches, out of reach from the bank, can be trimmed or tied back ready for when fishing commences.

Fish usually seem little concerned with the canoe, as long as the angler is quiet and still. They probably do not associate it with danger and regard it as just another weed raft drifting on the current. I have even seen a shoal priming all around the canoe as I drifted through it during an evening on the upper Wensum. When fish were caught later they turned out to be a mixture of dace and roach.

In 1980, I was fortunate to move into a cottage very close to the Wensum above

Launching a canoe onto the upper Wensum.

Costessey Mill. My land did not join the river but that of my neighbour did, running alongside and behind. The river is perhaps 150 yards from my boundary and it was only a matter of time before I was given permission to leave my canoe by the river, convenient for fishing trips whenever I liked. Now within minutes I can be afloat with the freedom of miles of river, much of it little fished, all to myself and the occasional kingfisher.

On many of Britain's rivers anglers and canoeists are often at loggerheads. Both sports make their demands on the water and have their extreme elements, but on occasion they have banded together to confront problems that deeply concern both parties, such as abstraction and the increase in motor boats. So there is hope for the future.

But it is not surprising that some anglers can only see canoes in a bad light, regarding them as a great disturbance and even a

A beautifully conditioned chub is displayed across the seat of the canoe.

damaging element where spawning grounds are concerned. I wonder, though, if the problem of disturbance is as bad as many anglers believe. Obviously a great number of canoes cannot be tolerated but I doubt whether a single canoe disturbs a swim for any great length of time. On the rivers that I fish in Norfolk canoeists are often encountered and I have found them to be respectful of anglers, sometimes gliding through the swim without paddling and even asking which side I would prefer them to pass on. Fish have been caught immediately after a canoe has been through, so proving the point. At least, that is my experience! I certainly have no reservations about fishing from a canoe.

The freedom of this style of fishing adds a new dimension to river fishing and is especially suited to those stretches where access is extremely difficult. It is also more suited to the less populated areas and I would not recommend it for the popular stretches where many bank anglers would be disturbed and friction would inevitably arise.

BOAT TYPE

My choice for this type of fishing is a large two-man Canadian canoe. I have used rowing boats but their wide, stubby design means that they are very difficult to row against the flow on some stretches of these upper rivers.

A canoe, being much more streamlined, cuts through the water with much less effort and disturbance. The paddle makes no noise at all in comparison with the creaking and clunking of a pair of oars, and the canoe glides effortlessly with steady alternating double strokes.

Contrary to popular belief, a canoe of this size is surprisingly stable, though standing is not advisable for any great length of time! The beam can be almost 3 feet on some

models and, although one angler is ideal, two anglers can fish in comfort provided their gear is kept to a minimum.

The majority of Canadian canoes are made in fibreglass and usually have very convenient storage compartments at the bows and stern in the otherwise wasted area where the craft narrows. These compartments, sometimes covered, are ideal for keeping cameras, small tackle bags and waterproofs tucked well away from the main area of the canoe.

One other main advantage with these canoes is their transportability. Being very light and manageable, they can be transported on almost any car roof. I have even seen them carried without a roof rack, the canoe simply tied on with only a section of foam or blanket to protect the paintwork of the car. Once the river is reached, the canoe can be carried or pulled the short distance to the water by one man with very little effort.

TACKLE AND ACCESSORIES

For a day on the river after chub and/or roach I would take the minimum of tackle. One small bag would contain cameras, a small tackle box, scales and weigh-bag; another would hold a selection of baits, flask and food. I usually take two rods, one set up for trotting with a centrepin, the other a quivertip rod for legering. A landing net completes the tackle, usually mounted on a short pole such as a bank stick.

A large foam cushion is useful not only to sit on but as an unhooking mat for anything that may come along. Fish are not retained unless especially noteworthy, and then only for a short period while cameras are made ready. Two small concrete mud weights are sometimes used for anchoring in midstream or in awkward swims, but not often. I generally prefer to tie up to bank-side vegetation or to use an anchor on the bank to keep the canoe stationary.

Stephen Harper trots for roach from a canoe using a centrepin.

FISH FINDING

As mentioned earlier, the close season is the ideal time and a canoe is the ideal method of fish location – the first rule of any form of angling.

As the spring and the close season draws to a close, the upper rivers are often in their best form for fish spotting. They have lost their thick winter colours and are fining down for the summer, though weed growth has yet to become fully established. To me this is the most enjoyable time of year for river watching as life returns after the long cold winter.

Several different species can often be observed spawning. The massing of the chub from all reaches of the river to the fast shallows at this time of year is awe-inspiring, as are the antics of the barbel, which throw all their usual caution to the wind with only one thought on their minds.

Once this annual ritual is over, the different species gradually filter back along the river to recuperate in the favourite deeper stretches and areas. This is the time to note the holding swims as the fish will often stay in roughly the same areas throughout the summer. This information is often still valid for winter fishing, as a good summer swim can be a good winter swim too.

A favourite way of locating chub during the summer and autumn is to cover the surface with floating crusts and follow them downstream in the canoe until fish are found. Nowadays on many of my favourite stretches it is difficult to hook fish consistently on floating crust, although they will take free offerings readily, so I use the system purely to locate some feeding fish and then trot or leger the area from the canoe. This may not be as exciting as catching them 'on the top', but often these methods are much more reliable.

LEGERING AND TROTTING

When legering you must take care to moor securely, though it is not as difficult to leger from a canoe as it would at first appear. With the rod laid across the canoe and the absence of a rod rest, bites, especially from chub, can be dramatic. The rod inititally twitches, then slams over and sometimes even slides along the gunwale before the strike is made.

The canoe really comes into its own for trotting, especially with a centrepin. If two anglers are aboard, the canoe must be anchored fore and aft across the flow. There is no need to cast; the floats are simply lowered into the water and line allowed to pay off as the trot is begun. With even the narrowest of rivers there is enough room for two to trot down, as long as strikes are made in opposite directions.

When fishing alone, I usually tie up to the left bank (looking downstream), the canoe parallel (and tied) to the bank. Being beyond marginal rushes, and just that bit further into the flow, there is once again no need to cast. The tackle can be either lowered or swung over to the far bank with only a single V of line taken from the centrepin. There is no need to use all your fingers to pull line off the reel for the cast, as you would from the bank.

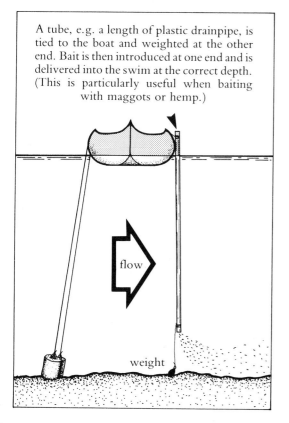

A tube, e.g. a length of plastic drainpipe, is tied to the boat and weighted at the other end. Bait is then introduced at one end and is delivered into the swim at the correct depth. (This is particularly useful when baiting with maggots or hemp.)

flow

weight

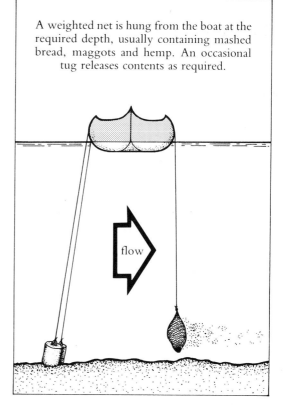

A weighted net is hung from the boat at the required depth, usually containing mashed bread, maggots and hemp. An occasional tug releases contents as required.

flow

Fig 11   Two methods of baiting a river swim from a canoe (shown here moored across the river).

BAITING THE SWIM

Whether legering or trotting for roach and chub, groundbait usually takes the form of mashed bread, sometimes laced with hemp, maggots and casters. This can be dispersed in several ways. It can be simply thrown in upstream, in the hope that it reaches bottom close to where your tackle is fishing. Or you can use the following more reliable methods to be sure that the groundbait does not disperse before it has reached bottom (though chub and roach will often take bait at any depth).

The first method is to use a weighted net full of mashed bread and any other additives you wish to include. This is hung directly beneath the canoe and every so often it is given a good tug to disperse some of its contents downstream at whatever depth it is hanging.

Another method, perhaps not so convenient, is to use a tube such as a length of drainpipe, sometimes with a funnel at the top. This tube is attached to the boat and weighted at one end. Groundbait is put into one end and comes out, dispersing at the required depth. Both these methods are very simple and very effective.

Chub, roach and dace are the main species that can be pursued from a canoe by the methods described. For the larger species such as pike and barbel I still have ambitions. I would love to catch a barbel in this manner

As darkness falls; a chub to trotted flake.

but I'm sure it would not be easy. And I would certainly have fun and games should it prove to be a fish of the size the Wensum is famous for.

Small pike have posed no real problems but a fast-water twenty from a canoe would, I am sure, be a fish to remember, possibly towing the canoe downstream if it was not moored securely. Still, it's a thought, and a new aim for the coming winter. So if you see an impressive bow-wave heading downstream towing a canoe containing a concerned-looking angler with rod well bent, you'll know who it is!

Punt Fishing for Bream

by Graham Marsden

Graham Marsden is one of Britain's best known and most successful anglers – not only for bream, on which he is arguably the country's leading authority, but for many other large fish of many species. He has lived in Cheshire all his life and has a great love of the countryside, in particular the meres and rivers that form such an important part of his angling.

As a regular contributor to the angling press, in particular the monthly magazines, his writings are respected by a wide cross-section of the angling community. He is also the author of the much-acclaimed book Advanced Coarse Fishing, *which aptly illustrates his wide knowledge and versatility.*

In this chapter Graham explains what an important part boats have played in his bream fishing, helping him to attain an enviable reputation, and he details the methods and tactics that have made him so successful.

SH

Fishing from a sturdy flat-bottomed punt can be one of the most exhilarating experiences in an angler's career – that is, if he goes about it the right way, for if he doesn't it can be the most disastrous thing he will ever do. Without sensible safety measures it can be fatal.

REFINEMENTS

The basic design of punts is pretty standard and need not concern us here. What I will tell you about are some of the refinements with which my pal Eric Barnes and I equip our punts.

At strategic points we bolt tubes on the sides to take an umbrella. There are four of these so that no matter which side of the punt we fish from there is a brolly tube behind our left shoulder. A left-handed angler will, of course, need the tube behind his right shoulder.

The floor-boards have laths nailed around the edge. The function of these is simply to prevent your chair from slipping off, which, at best, will frighten the fish and, at worst, will flip you over the side, both frightening the fish and possibly resulting in more serious consequences.

The floor-boards are covered with tough, hard-wearing low-pile carpets. These serve the purpose of providing a soft base on which to unhook fish, and to dampen the noise of careless feet and dropped objects. Punts emphasise noise; they're like buoyant drums. These carpets, of course, get wet. But who cares? Soaking wet they serve exactly the same purpose.

At one end of the punt is a covered section, which is ideal for stowing camera bags and other delicate or otherwise vulnerable objects when there is a sudden downpour, or to protect them from harsh sunlight and heat.

Around the edge of the punt is pipe insulation. This tubular foam has been slit

Eric Barnes displays a large, two-tone bream caught in mirror-calm conditions.
Photo: Graham Marsden

down its length and prised open to slot over the edge and left to self-grip. This way it can easily be replaced as it gets worn or damaged. The foam prevents knocks and abrasions to rods and also deadens noise.

AN ELECTRIC OUTBOARD

The best investment Eric and I ever made, following the acquisition of a punt, was an outboard motor. There is only one thing worse than trying to row or punt out to a distant swim against a strong wind and choppy surface, and that's trying to row or punt back to the bank. At least on the way out you have enthusiasm to drive you on.

On a large water of upwards of 200 acres a petrol-driven outboard is probably the best answer, providing club rules allow one.

And there is no reason why an outboard motor should disturb the fish if you use it moderately and carefully, and row the last forty yards or so to the swim.

Best of all, though, is an electric outboard motor. They're almost silent, easy to use and, most important, pollution-free. Ours, of Shakespeare manufacture, runs off an ordinary 12-volt car battery and has a maximum thrust of 38 pounds, which comfortably drives our snub-nosed flat-bottomed punt through the most severe water – on one occasion through 'white-horse'-capped waves we really had no right to be out in but which whipped up quite suddenly and caught us by surprise.

The Shakespeare motor has five forward speeds and five reverse, and can be attached very easily to almost any type of transom. It is relatively light and convenient to carry

A bream of over 9lb caught by Eric Barnes. This picture also shows the Shakespeare electric outboard and battery.

Photo: Graham Marsden

around, lighter in fact than the 12-volt battery that provides the power. Demonstrate the motor to controlling clubs and/or riparian owners and all but the most intransigent will allow their use. A motor, electric or petrol, makes boat fishing more of a pleasure and less of a chore.

ANCHORING

Punts require anchoring in one way or another. If you are fishing from marginal reed-mace, or a reed-mace island, then you need do no more than tie up at each end to a bunch of reed-mace stems.

In deep water anchors are required, one at each end of the punt. Numerous objects can be used as anchors, for you don't need anything elaborate to provide sufficient grip in silt and mud or soft sand. I use a plastic sweet bottle filled with concrete, with an eye bolt sunk into the top. When the plastic bottle eventually cracks and breaks away it doesn't matter, for you're still left with a concrete anchor. The bottle is really only a mould.

When you've found a swim you know you will be fishing regularly it is best to leave the anchors in the swim, rather than hauling them in and out of the punt on every visit. All you need to do is tie a plastic bottle (an empty 2-litre orange-juice bottle is ideal), part-filled with water, to the anchor rope and leave it to float on the surface.

In shallower water it is better to sink in a

FEEDING ROUTES

Right, let's go fishing for bream from a punt. The punt gives us a tremendous advantage, in that otherwise inaccessible areas become accessible, and bream that previously had to be legered for, because of the feeding route's great distance from the bank, are now open to any method we care to choose, particularly float fishing with light and sensitive tackle.

From a boat, as from the bank, first principles always apply, and the first task before we do anything else is to locate the feeding grounds of the bream. For this a boat gives us a great advantage. It means that we can moor the boat anywhere on the water that gives us a clear view of certain areas of the lake, for the best way of locating bream is actually to see them priming along those underwater freeways we know as patrol routes. Bream have the very useful habit of rolling at the surface at odd points over the track, or beat, along which they feed. A boat also allows us to get close enough to see the bubbles and mud clouds they produce when feeding. This means that bream don't have to roll to give away their presence, which is sometimes the case on one or two waters, though waters where the bream do not roll are the exception rather than the rule.

The most likely time for seeing bream roll is in the early morning or late evening, with early morning – from an hour before to a couple of hours after daybreak – the best of all. It would be a wise investment to spend a few early mornings on your chosen water, moored at various strategic points, and make notes of where you see bream roll. On a large water there will likely be several shoals, and you will find that there is a pattern in their feeding behaviour, both in the routes along which they feed and the times they feed at. With binoculars you can scan the water for bubbles and other signs of

Early morning action as a bream is played towards the punt.

Photo: Graham Marsden

stake at each end of the punt and tie up to them. Scaffolding poles make good stakes, but you have to be careful not to sink them in so far that you cannot get them out again. I've seen it happen. Tying up to firm stakes is by far the best way of holding the punt stationary, for no matter how tight you get anchor ropes there is always some degree of swing, the exact amount depending on the length of the anchor ropes, which is dictated by the depth of the water.

If you are float fishing, a reasonable amount of swing is acceptable, for it will not affect your fishing. But, if you wish to leger, then punt movements must be kept to an absolute minimum, and stakes are essential, unless, of course, the water is shallow enough to use long rod rests outside the punt.

feeding, but always with the thought that other fish, especially tench, could be the cause of the activity.

When you have located a feeding route, note particularly where the route veers off at a tangent and/or comes to an end. These turning points and terminal points, as I call them, are usually the hot spots and are always, respectively, my first and second choice of swim.

My ideal swim is a feeding route that ends at the base of a ledge. Such a swim has several very valuable advantages, especially when it can be fished from a punt. The terminal point and the ledge combine to provide a swim that bream love and will feed in for long periods. The ledge, and this is very important if we are to float fish at fairly close range, offers cover for us, for if we anchor the punt fifteen yards or so back from the top of the ledge we will be out of sight of the bream, which will feed some-where down the slope or at the bottom of the drop-off. The punt will probably be in shallow water which allows us to stake it firmly or anchor with short ropes.

SWIM PREPARATION

The next thing to do is bait the swim as often as possible before you fish – at least three or four times a week for a couple of weeks to have the most telling effect. Try to prebait at the same time you will be feeding the swim when you begin to fish. But pre-baiting at any time of day or night is better than not prebaiting at all.

You must, of course, prebait with what-ever you intend to use as hookbait, and the best baits for bream are maggot, caster, sweetcorn and worm. Bread is also a very good bream bait but is prone to producing bites that are difficult to hit.

The question of how much you should introduce when prebaiting is similar to

Graham Marsden returns a very large bream from the punt.

Photo: Graham Marsden

asking 'How long is a piece of string?' It varies, of course, from one water to another, depending on the number of fish in the water, the number and size of the shoals that visit the swim, and many other factors. The only answer is trial and error, but it is better to feed too little than too much. Of the baits I've mentioned, casters and sweetcorn are best for prebaiting. Both are inert and will therefore lie in the swim until they're con-sumed. Casters are a supreme bait for bream of any size, while sweetcorn is specially good for specimen bream.

TACKLE AND RIGS

When bream fishing from a punt with float tackle you don't need to fish heavy, even if the bream run into double figures. But you

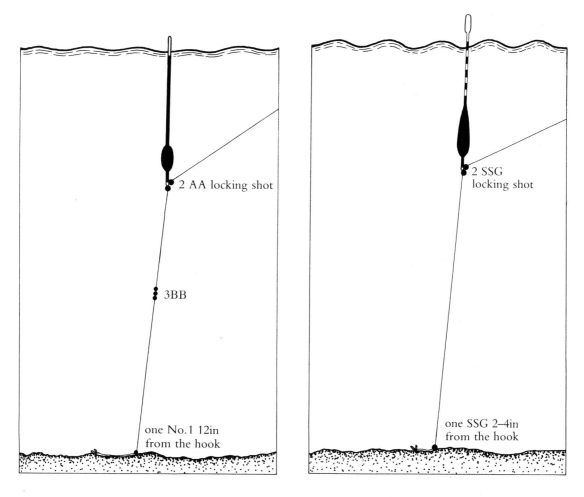

Fig 12   (a) Bodied waggler float rig   (b) Drennan 'Driftbeater' float rig.

must use balanced tackle. My choice is a 12-foot or 13-foot match rod and a reel line of 2½-pound test, either straight through or tied to a 2-pound bottom. I generally fish it straight through to begin with and only go finer if I find it necessary.

Hook size depends on the bait I'm using. I fish a size 10 with lobworm, a 12 with corn and a 14 with maggot, caster and redworm. There are many occasions, however, when I have to reduce my hook size to a 16 or even an 18 for maggot or caster when the bream are being finicky.

I generally use one of two types of float when bream fishing from a punt. When the punt is staked quite firmly and the water's surface is very choppy I prefer the Drennan 'Driftbeater' (*see* Fig 12b). As its name suggests, it is an excellent float for beating drift and a rough surface. It registers lift bites as no other float can, providing of course that the float is set up correctly. Unfortunately, few anglers know how to fish the lift method, for the principle is so different from conventional float techniques.

To begin with, it is essential – not simply

advisable, but *essential* – that a large shot is used on the bottom. This should be an SSG, and be no more than 4 inches from the hook.

The principle is that this heavy bottom shot holds the float down (with the assistance of the locking shot) almost to the sight bob. Then the rod is rested and the line tightened until only the sight bob remains above surface. If you have got it right the float will be almost straining to rise out of the water – as it surely will as soon as a fish sucks in the bait and disturbs that bottom shot.

My second choice of float, when conditions are somewhat calmer, is a bodied waggler, shotted as in Fig 12a, with no more than ¼ inch showing above surface. The shot sizes shown are an example only, for there is a wide variety and size of bodied waggler floats which in different conditions, will demand different sizes of shot.

FEEDING A SWIM

I have already said that the greatest advantage a punt gives you is access to areas out of reach of the bank angler, and being able to float fish with highly sensitive tackle. I could be wrong, for another tremendous advantage, perhaps even more valuable, is being able to loose feed, little and often.

Bream, like most fish, but particularly bream, being shoal fish, and hungry ones at that, are subject to preoccupation. If an angler can get a shoal of fish preoccupied with the bait he is using he would have to try very hard not to make a big catch.

It is far easier to preoccupy a shoal with your hookbait if you can catapult that hookbait freely into the swim without the hindrance and handicap of groundbait as a carrying agent to distant swims.

Loose feeding means you can have hook-

John Charleswoth, in amongst the bulrushes, with an Irish bream from Lough Ree.
Photo: Graham Marsden

Heading out to a swim on a large reservoir that would be inaccessible from the bank.
Photo: Graham Marsden

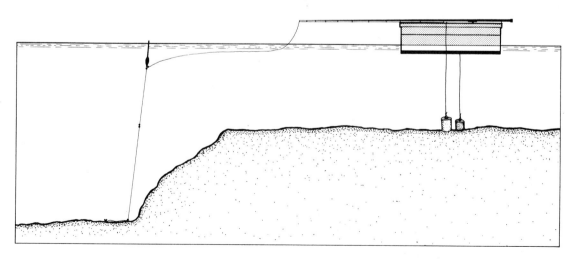

Fig 13   Punt anchored over shallow water. Bait float-fished at foot of ledge.

bait sinking into the swim almost continually, even if it means firing no more than a dozen casters, say, every twenty seconds. You can create a rhythm that provides the bream, continually, with just enough loose feed to keep them interested and constantly prodding around for more. Not too much, not too little – that's the secret.

Many times you will drive the fish into coming off the bottom to intercept loose feed as it sinks. But that's no problem when float fishing; you simply adjust your shotting until your hookbait behaves in exactly the same manner.

I do occasionally leger for bream from a punt, but only when I'm fishing a water – probably with exceptionally big fish – that produces very few bites. It is a far more relaxing form of fishing. You can watch the water for fish, or admire the bird life, and know that a bite alarm will warn you when a bite does come. Otherwises I prefer to float fish, from the comfort and stability of a well-equipped punt.

Carp Fishing and Inflatable Boats

by John Webb

John Webb has fished for many years but for the last six seasons he has concentrated on carp to the exclusion of all other species. A member of the Carp Society and regional organiser for the Doncaster area, he has written several articles for the society's high-quality magazine, Carp Fisher. *He is perhaps unusual as a carp angler in that rather than sitting it out for only a few big fish he would rather catch many more carp of a smaller size, with the outside chance of something weightier.*

John has made the inflatable dinghy an integral part of much of his carp fishing and as this chapter reveals, this has led to many more carp being netted than would have been possible by using more conventional methods.

SH

This chapter is not about how to fish for carp from a boat, it is about how to use a boat to enhance your carp fishing. Dealing mainly with the placement of bait, it chronicles my experience and gives details of the methods used and the reasoning behind them.

The use of boats in carp fishing is rather controversial. I do not intend to be controversial, nor do I condone those who use boats without any consideration for their fellow anglers. Where the rules specifically forbid the use of boats, don't use them. However, don't be surprised if a quiet word with the owner or the bailiff doesn't turn out to your advantage.

Boats are banned on many mixed fisheries, especially those run by clubs. If you are fortunate enough to fish a club water where boats are not banned, one sure way to get them banned is to row out in the middle of the annual 'Joe Bloggs Memorial Match'. Discretion is the name of the game, if not plain secrecy. Carp anglers used to be a secretive lot and we were probably better off that way in some respects.

My involvement with boats began in the close season of 1980 when I took the club rowing-boat round the local brickyard pond, which is a maze of islands, channels, weed beds and snags. It was a calm, sunny afternoon and I found some carp basking, backs out of the water, in amongst a reed bed. I was amazed that the carp showed no signs of fear as I eased the boat slowly through the reeds. I could get as close as two feet before they waddled off and settled a couple of yards to the side.

'D' LAKE, WAVENEY

It wasn't until July 1983 that I used a boat in order to catch carp. The place was the famous Waveney Valley caravan-park complex. It was my first visit to the complex. I was fishing 'C' lake, the sun was very hot and none of the lakes was fishing too well. Over on 'D' lake, though, the lads in swims 1 and 2 were caning the carp. One of these blokes, Graham Cowderoy, had had over

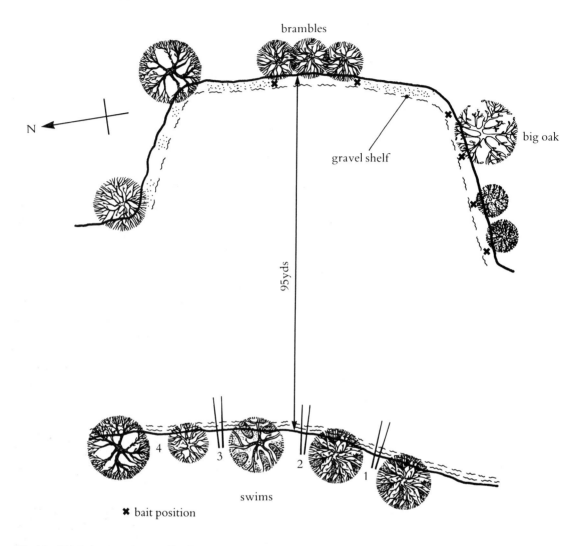

Fig 14 'D' Lake, Waveney Valley Complex.

thirty fish during the previous week with the biggest weighing in at thirty-one pounds nine ounces. They were definitely doing something right. They were fishing into the margins of the spit that separates 'D' and 'E' lakes and they were using the boat to do it. The boat used to be a fixture at Waveney; it was used to free snagged fish and to remove the nuisance line that adorned the branches all along the spit. (These uses are probably the best advantages to point out to an owner or bailiff when trying to obtain permission to use a boat.) Graham explained that they were placing their hookbaits tight in the margins, under the overhanging trees, and baiting heavily with boilies. 'They're having it because they've never seen baits there before,' he said.

On the second night, Graham took me out in the boat to show me what he was doing. All along the margin of the spit was a narrow gravel shelf about two feet down; you could feel it with the oar. Much of this shelf is impossible to cast to, because of the overhanging trees. At my request, we traced the shelf around the back bay up to the trailing brambles. Here the shelf was about four feet wide.

I moved into swim 3 on 'D' lake as soon as it fell vacant, made up a load of boilies and got into the boat. I placed my hookbaits about eighteen inches from the bank at each end of the trailing bramble hedge. I then scattered about 300 boilies all along the shelf in front of the brambles. It was the last day of my stay, so I was only in the swim for about twenty-four hours. I had three runs though, and landed two of them – one was a personal best. After each run, I rowed out a fresh hookbait and scattered a further 100 or so boilies around it. Mine were the first fish to be caught outside swims 1 and 2 for ten days, and that is a long time at Waveney.

As I've mentioned, it was very hot and the carp seemed to be spending most of the time in the upper layers of the water. By presenting our baits perfectly on the shelf we were effectively fishing in the upper layers. I'm not sure if Graham's theory of putting baits where the carp had never seen them works or not; I was fishing the shelf at a point where it could be cast to. However, trying to hit a four-foot-wide strip, up against a bramble hedge, is no easy matter.

The following year, I purchased a small inflatable dinghy and used similar tactics almost every time I fished at Waveney. I never blanked, often at times when everybody else did. The method didn't just work when the weather is hot. At the end of the 1984/5 season I caught my biggest Waveney fish on a pop-up over a tight bed of maple peas under the first branch of the big oak on 'D' lake. I am sure that the fish became accustomed to finding food and visited the area all year round.

HOMERSFIELD LAKE

In 1985 I became a member of the Homersfield syndicate. I was very excited; from the tales I'd heard, it was reputed to be absolutely stacked with carp from single figures through to thirty-five pounds plus. Although Homersfield is practically next door to Waveney, it is a very different lake. It is situated in a hollow in the middle of a low hill and this makes it very sheltered – seemingly cut off from the rest of the world. The lake is about thirty acres in size and has several large islands. These give the lake an intimacy which is usually found only on smaller waters.

I took my dinghy with me, but didn't need it at first. The carp would feed almost anywhere and the closest you needed to cast to the islands was about three yards – there was no shelf as at Waveney. Boilies could be (and were) catapulted to just about anywhere on the lake.

John Webb with a 21lb 4oz Homersfield carp that fell to maize accurately placed by inflatable dinghy.
Photo: John Webb

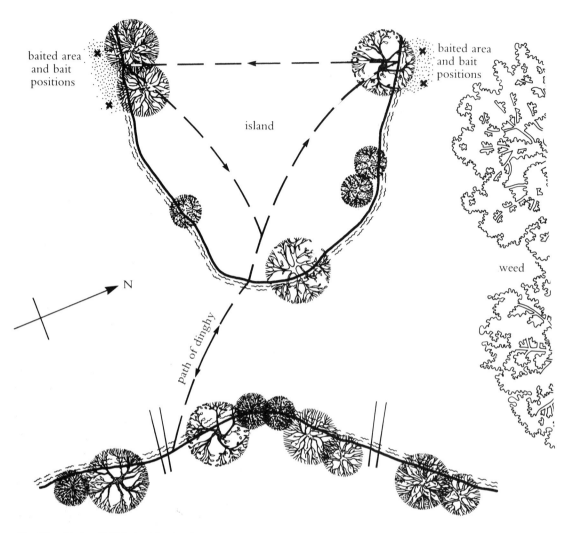

baited area
and bait
positions

baited area
and bait
positions

island

N

weed

path of dinghy

Fig 15 Homersfield Lake island swims.

The first problem that cropped up at Homersfield was the weed. There was hardly any at the start of the season, but about the beginning of July the stuff started growing at about two feet a day. It was incredible: one day I was landing every fish I hooked; the next day every one was getting weeded. We devised a system for freeing snagged fish, using the dinghy. This improved the situation immensely and I went from losing 75 per cent of the fish hooked to landing 75 per cent. Ideally, you need someone to help you, because taking the rod and landing net out on your own is not very wise. I found this out to my cost on 'G' lake at Waveney; I nearly sank when a fish towed me into some brambles. Get someone to hold your rod while you get into your boat. Pull yourself out along the snagged line (I've done this with lines as low as 5-pound BS) and eventually you will be directly over the fish. Firmly, but gently, pull the line directly upwards; be very ready to ease off as soon as you feel the fish moving. You will be successful 90 per cent of the time and the fish will come up easily. I have never snapped off, but I have pulled out of a few. If it is very weedy, get the man on the rod to tow

The best of the week at Homersfield, Bev's 24lb 1oz two-tone beauty.

Photo: John Webb

you in while you keep the fish clear of the weed on a short line. Controlling a fish on a short handline is not easy, though. When you are ready, warn the man on the rod, then release your hold on the line carefully so as to prevent the line snatching at the hookhold. You can then row back to the bank and resume playing the fish normally. People have commented that the fish don't stand a chance, but I'm not in the business of giving any carp the chance to injure or even kill itself by towing yards of line around.

Incidentally, I've been realiably informed that the carp in the French Lake Cassien are becoming increasingly wary of boats. Could they be associating them with danger due to the fact that many of the carp are being played from, and landed into, boats? Perhaps my method is an improvement.

Homersfield is very heavily stocked, but

it became apparent that at any one time, up to 90 per cent of the carp would be holed up in a comparatively small area, and they would use the same holding area for much of the season. This area could be covered by no more than five swims and obviously those swims were very much in demand. If you were lucky enough to get into one of them, you could catch very large bags by simply casting out hookbaits on their own. The carp were in the area and they were staying there. Their sheer numbers meant that even the small percentage that made a mistake made for excellent fishing.

Every now and then, large shoals of up to 100 carp would leave the holding area and go on the feed, covering large areas in a very short time. In most of the swims at Homersfield you had to be content with picking off fish from these roving shoals as they passed through. The best swims were those with obstacles such as islands or bars in them, where a concentration of carp would occur. Very heavy baiting was best in order to slow the fish down a bit and increase your chances. The most bait you could reasonably make on your own was about 13 pounds of boilies (12 eggs). This amount could be introduced in two or three batches; the action would come in fast bursts of up to an hour, and you would get from one to four runs two or three times per day. It was obvious that the bait was being rapidly cleared and the carp were moving on. Sometimes you just knew that it was all gone after only a few minutes.

In order to prolong the action, I knew that I would have to use particles. The problem was that, except for sweetcorn, all particles were banned – and the huge Homersfield roach just loved sweetcorn. I decided to use maize, as it is cheaper than frozen or tinned corn and it is easier to keep. However, it does take an overnight soak and twenty minutes in the pressure-cooker to soften it.

At the start of the following season I

obtained unofficial permission from the bailiffs to use the dinghy for baiting up – provided I was discreet, as they weren't sure that the owner would approve.

At first the results were disappointing. I was putting about six pounds per night in but only getting three or four runs a day. However, on the third session of the season I settled into a quiet swim on a point at the eastern end of the lake. In front and slightly to the left of the swim is a large island. There is a large bush overhanging the margins of the island about forty-five yards out. It is the sort of swim that just screams CARP! The swim has the added convenience that the island blocks the view from the rest of the lake, which allowed me to take the boat out at any time. Putting maize in regularly, a pressure-cooker load (three to four pounds) at a time, I took eleven carp to eighteen pounds ten ounces in thirty-six hours. This was more like it!

I had been noting down everything I had done: weather, the time I was putting bait in, the time of runs, which rod, which rig, and so on. When I got home, I analysed my results and this is what I found:

1.   It made no difference whether I used mono or dacron, so I decided to use mono and get less tangles.
2.   Ordinary (rather than pop-up) boilies on a 10-inch bare-hook rig (size 4) produced more runs than any other combination tried.
3.   Most important, I never had any action more than two hours after putting a panload of maize in, nor did I get more than three runs per panload. I decided to go for bust and put a panload in every two hours or every three runs, whichever came first. This meant that I might be putting up to eight panloads in per day. I had no intention of putting any bait in at night.

I went down for a weekend in mid-August and got into a routine that was hard work, but very rewarding and enjoyable. I cooked a pan of maize, cooled it down in the water and put it in a bag in the dinghy, then I reeled in and rebaited both rods. After rowing out and baiting up a 3 x 5 yard rectangle next to the bush, I recast both rods and put another pan of maize on.

Over the fifty or so hours of the session, the carp practically threw themselves at me. I was using foam in the buttring and I had so much action that the line cut the foam in half. I ended up putting about twenty-eight pounds of maize in per day and, if you are into numbers, I had twenty-six runs, landed nineteen, eight of which were over fifteen pounds and the biggest was a chunky twenty-pound fourteen-ounce mirror. I only had two runs at night – good job too, as I needed a rest.

Two weeks later, I returned to the same swim. This time my wife, Bev, fished the swim on the other side of the point, from where she could mirror my tactics on the other side of the island.

Over the week, we took more than forty carp between us, my best weighing twenty-one pounds four ounces and Bev's twenty-four pounds one ounce. The action was much less intense than my previous session and I put this down to two main reasons: all week the wind was blowing over our heads to the far end of the lake; and, more significantly, we had to share the bait, and eight panloads per day was all we could cook with one pressure-cooker. Nonetheless, between us we caught as many carp as the rest of the syndicate who were there that week. It was absolutely magic fishing.

THE HORSESHOE LAKE

Whilst I was at Homersfield I began to hear about a very prolific water where about one

Fantastic, fully scaled mirrors from the Horseshoe Lake held by Bev and Jon the bailiff.
Photo: John Webb

in three of the stock are fully-scaled mirrors. It was called Horseshoe Lake. I was really getting into catching lots of carp and I've always wanted to catch a double-figure fully-scaled mirror, so I rang one of the bailiffs for some information. There is a yacht club on Horseshoe, which is a very large lake of eighty-four acres, who have exclusive boating rights. However, I managed to obtain unofficial permission to bait up with the dinghy between the hours of 8 p.m. and 8 a.m. when the sailors weren't around. Jon, the bailiff, advised me to use tiger nuts, but I decided to stick with maize – especially as it is only a fifth of the cost of tigers.

In October, Bev and I made our first trip down to Horseshoe, choosing the big double swim next to the disabled anglers' point.

We had been warned that it was a very weedy lake and this does tend to put some anglers off. However, after a bit of casting around we soon found a fairly clear strip about fifty yards out and parallel with our bank. I plumbed the area as best I could (which is not easy in weed) and found that it was about eight feet deep, and not a bar as we had thought at first. We made up some markers out of ET polyballs (1¼ inch) tied slightly over depth to a lump of lead. I had used these black and orange balls before and they are easily visible up to about 150 yards. I tend to rely heavily on emergent features for accuracy and I've come up with a fairly foolproof method of placing markers. I cast out to wherever I wish to bait up, row out along the line (put the anti-reverse on) until I reach the lead. Then I throw the marker a

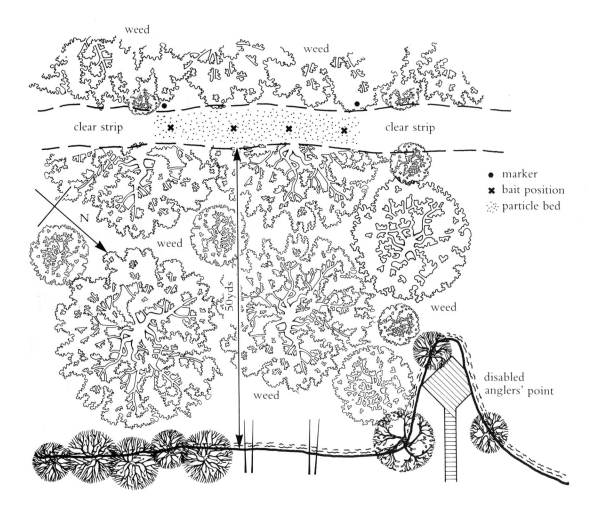

weed

weed

clear strip · x · x · x · x · clear strip

N

weed

• marker
✖ bait position
⋯ particle bed

50yds

weed

weed

weed

disabled
anglers' point

Fig 16   The Horseshoe Lake.

couple of yards further out. Don't drop the marker where you intend to place a bait as you'll end up getting tangled.

It is amazing how quickly you drift in a small dinghy, so I use an anchor – mine is a brick tied to about 14 feet of strong nylon chord. Tie this behind you in the boat and you will always settle with your back to the wind; this reduces any tendency to spin when you are throwing bait out. If you approach your marker from upwind and drop the anchor when you are about five yards away, you will settle in a perfect

position from which you can place bait in a 3 x 8 yard rectangle.

We started putting maize in, seven pounds at a time, morning and night. By the end of the week we were averaging two runs a day each, although I must point out that Bev had twice as many runs as I did. We both caught our fully-scaled mirrors, Bev's best being sixteen pounds five ounces. However, I wasn't satisfied; I felt that we would have caught more if we had put more bait in.

I didn't return until the following June, the second week of the season. We went

Another fully scaled mirror from the Horseshoe Lake at just over 15lb.

Photo: John Webb

John's wife Bev shows off the classic symmetry of a long mirror from the Horseshoe Lake.

Photo: John Webb

into the same swim and fished as before, but with fourteen pounds of maize going in twice a day, along a line about fifteen yards long and three yards wide. It was quite a struggle getting into the dinghy with the anchor and a big carrier bag of maize, but it was well worth the effort. At the end of four days we had used up a 25-kilo sack of maize and had about thirty runs – my best being a fantastic seventeen-pound eleven-ounce fully-scaled mirror. We'd had about twice the action for twice the bait, but the weather was bad. It was rcd-hot sun and no wind. Things could only get better.

Two further four-day sessions in August and September were better. The weather was perfect on both occasions and we averaged eleven runs a day between us, even though we rarely bothered to recast after dark.

SUMMARY

There are five main uses for boats in carp fishing:

1. Freeing snagged or weeded fish.
2. Clearing nuisance line, etc., from trees overhanging your swim.
3. Exploring your swim – finding bars and so on.
4. Placing hookbaits (and free offerings) up against margins or snags at distance or night.
5. Placing very large beds of particle bait beyond effective catapult range.

I have tried similar tactics to those at Horseshoe by using a bait dropper on waters where boats are banned. In order to achieve similar levels of action, you end up bait-dropping for about four hours each day. This just does not compare to twenty minutes in a dinghy and your arms don't feel like dropping off as they do after a dropping stint.

Finally, a word or two about safety. The best dinghies are double-skinned, which is handy when you have to go near brambles. I prefer to use a very small dinghy and people have commented that it doesn't look very stable. Actually, it is like sitting in a large inner tube (with a bottom) and it is hard enough to get out of when you want to, let alone fall out.

The Boat in Tench Fishing

by Roger Miller

When not fishing, Roger Miller is a Norfolk policeman, but he is probably best known for his exploits with the huge roach of the upper Wensum. He is one of the few anglers to have caught a roach of over 3 pounds. He also enjoys fishing for rudd, bream, pike and perch. While recent summers have been spent in pursuit of big tench, he has recently succumbed to the spell of the ferox of Scotland's lochs.

    Roger has co-authored two books with John Bailey: Bream – Tales and Tactics *and* Perch. *He writes regularly for the angling monthlies. In this chapter he describes his exploits afloat after the tench of Upton Broad and details his tactics and methods for achieving total stability whilst legering from a boat.*

SH

Among my earliest inspirations on deciding to pursue Norfolk's larger tench were the many private enclosed broads that had never seen a cruiser – land-locked domain of aged boat-houses and impenetrable marsh and acres of alder, willow and oak; clear-water havens of lily and sedge, with dark black shapes rolling at dusk far out in the middle, safe from anglers restricted to the old stagings.

The lovely old shooting punt, last used fifteen years earlier in the 1970s, lay rotten and abandoned. Great breaming feats had been witnessed upon her and it was sad to see the old punt slowly rotting into the marshy bank, and with her so much history. It was with bream in mind that I eased the canoe across the reflected sky and out into the centre of the most beautiful broad I have ever fished – Upton.

Late May, and the early evening was laden with humidity and languid, stifling air. The sun, creeping towards the edge of the big Norfolk sky, plunged its beams down into the clear waters of the broad at the deep eastern end. Ignoring the melancholy of that beautiful but decaying place, the courting grebes and the hordes of mallard, the eerie presence of the capsized and decaying boat, scene of a tragic drowning in the 1930s, even ignoring the giant silhouettes of the bream fleeing at my approach, it was the sudden discovery of tench that had the most profound effect upon me. Let me tell you how I stumbled into their sanctum.

I nearly missed the bay, almost another broad, and I was sure that everybody else had too. I had never heard anything of it, and my entry into it had the same effect as a fox entering a chicken coop. Am I alone in my penchant for suddenly bursting through the undergrowth, stumbling through the tangled thicket, through the pollen-choking haze of an abandoned ley to find an aquatic environment so blissful yet lost and obscured, so tiny and unremarkable that all others ignore it?

As I slipped the canoe through the narrow channel the tench at first just carried on sucking the bloodworms out of the silt. As

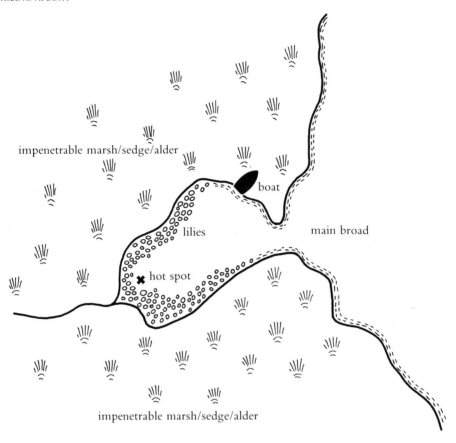

Fig 17   The Bay swim.

the canoe moved closer there was hell to pay, for big, black old tench charged into the sedge, up and down and eventually out of their hitherto uncharted sanctuary. Thought of the bream, for which the broad was justly famous, evaporated, and in its place came a surge of desire to boat some of these truly wild unheard-of Broadland tench.

My initial evening-to-dawn session in this bay was a failure, and it was not until I was rowing back that I realised why. Stupidly, I had moored the boat in the entrance to the bay, and the tench, not being resident, were evidently unhappy at having to swim beneath it in order to enter and feed.

When I arrived back at the farm by the broad that morning at least a dozen hens were roosting on the car, parked in the barn

the night before. As I enjoyed the tea offered by the family I realised that my summer would be spent there – afloat.

The following evening I moored the boat in the bay with the aid of long poles. All the enclosed broads I have fished are badly silted, with several feet of silt often lying on a firmer base. Upton is no exception. Mud weights, while adequate for most pike fishing situations on these broads, are useless for pursuing such fish as tench, when bite indication and rigidity of the boat are of prime importance. The mud weights rest deep in the silt but the ropes obviously cannot hold the boat solid in the water. One cannot afford even the tiniest movement of the boat when legering or float fishing in a sensitive manner, such as the lift method.

Roger Miller returns a tench to Upton Broad.
Photo: Roger Miller

In contrast to his tenching exploits, Roger Miller in colder climes afloat.
Photo: Martyn Page

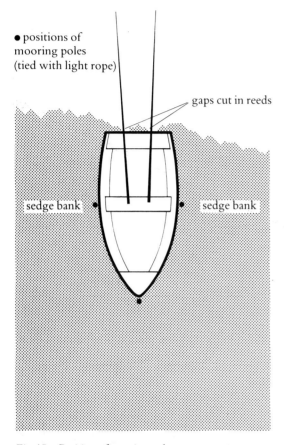

● positions of
mooring poles
(tied with light rope)

gaps cut in reeds

sedge bank

sedge bank

Fig 18   Position of mooring poles.

So, with the longest poles I could muster from the boat-house, I rowed across to the bay and moored the boat within easy casting distance of the hot spot. But once again I failed. The advantage of being able to fish the bay with the aid of a boat was lost when the boat frightened the previously undisturbed tench. With the bay surrounded by thick beds of sedge, I thought of a possible solution. I moored the boat *in* the sedge, cutting narrow gaps to allow the rods to protrude through. Adopting the wildfowler's approach, I created a hide of sorts and by leaving the poles in position I could move the boat in and out of the hide with the minimum of disturbance. My preparations

even ran to painting the black hull of the boat a rich green to blend in with the sedge bank even better.

Always, when boat fishing, my prime objective is to make the boat into a rigid, firm and, if at all possible, invisible 'bank'. I am convinced that predators such as pike and perch can actually be attracted by a boat if it is moored for long enough, unlike the cyprinids, which remain terrified of it, especially in shallow crystal-clear broads. Fig 19 shows my set-up in the boat itself. It is a simple matter to attach two Betalite bobbins to act as bite indicators, thereby transforming fishing from a boat into a method as practical as fishing from the bank.

With the boat hidden, and the set-up as outlined, I began to enjoy some of the most aesthetically pleasing fishing I have ever known. The water was clear, the lilies lush and emerald-green. Golden shapes tipped up as they meandered through the entangled stems to sip at corn. The world was lost as I sat in that boat surrounded by a sea of flapping green stems with the occasional explosion of sound as at last a tench made its mistake.

It did not take long before the two lines entering the water caused the tench to fret, especially when they brushed against them. A quick change to a float, fished slightly over depth, extended my dawns of success in the bay. The set-up within the boat stayed the same as for legering. Predictably, however, the pressure I was bringing to bear on the tiny bay was beginning to have an effect. The small band of tench were becoming increasingly neurotic and I realised that I had to move out into the main broad. Until then the fishing had been easy. The real test for my approach was at hand.

As the angle of the sun's rays began to flood the bay with harsh light, forcing the long shapes of gold to vacate, I followed them for a short way, losing them suddenly

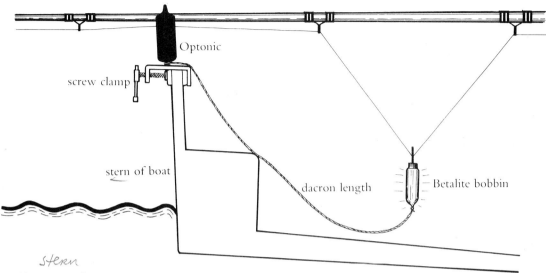

Optonic

screw clamp

stern of boat

dacron length

Betalite bobbin

Fig 19 Front rod rest set-up.

stern
∧

A 5lb 3oz tench taken by Martyn Page during a typical 'tench' dawn.
Photo: Martyn Page

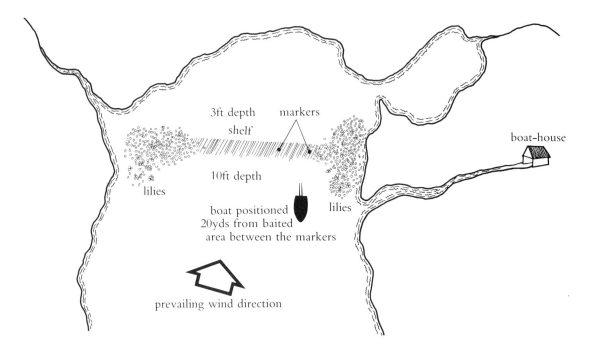

Fig 20   The 'Shelf' swim.

as they disappeared over a shelf as dramatic as any I had seen in a gravel pit. Different tactics would be called for now as I had to fish in the middle of the broad but maintain the same degree of sensitivity. The new swim lacked the intimacy of the bay but a new challenge lay ahead, so it was with a new optimism that I moored the boat over the shelf and scattered a couple of cans of corn directly over the area I hoped would produce another string of big tench. Among my most important items of tackle when boat fishing in this way are two highly visible pike bungs anchored by large bombs over the baited area to act as markers. It is so easy to lose your bearings afloat. To line baited areas up against landmarks is not accurate enough for me. Try both methods and you will soon see the superiority of the markers. If nobody else is fishing the water it is a good idea to leave both markers in place so the fish become used to them, and not least because you will be able to bait up

without having to row the boat over the swim. Twenty yards is a good distance to moor away from the baited area but still close enough to afford comfortable, easy fishing.

The bow of the boat should always be facing upwind so that the wind is split and its effect on the rigidity of the boat is reduced. Fig 21 shows the exact set-up I favour as I believe it is important to know precisely where everything is, especially at night.

A total of five extremely long straight poles are vital and in this case I decided to leave poles A, B, C and D in place between sessions in order to avoid noise when setting up. The poles *had* to be driven as deeply as possible into the silt so that the boat could be tied to them without any movement whatsoever whilst fishing, and this required no less than a large lump hammer. Pole E was the only removable pole and this allowed me to row the boat stern first into the 'park'

1. Landing net
2. Carpet tacked to
   stern gunwale
3. Optonics
4. Oars
5. Carpeting for
   unhooking
6. Forceps

7. Bait tins
8. Torch
9. Scales
10. Carpeting to avoid
    vibrations
11. Tackle bag
● A, B, C, D Poles
E Bow pole is removable

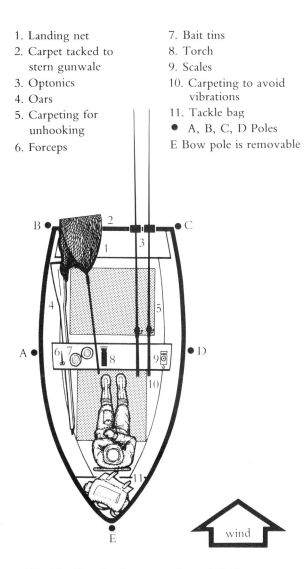

Fig 21   Complete boat set-up for tench fishing.

Optonic was caused by movement of the boat. I was quite confident in hitting the slightest twitch to the bobbin, knowing it to be a fish and not the boat. Many of these twitches were missed, unfortunately, but many were converted into fine tench of between five and seven pounds. This fact alone is enough to justify my elaborate preparations, but there is another.

Much of my fishing these days takes place on extremely large Highland lochs. Two Highland friends have done a lot of work by diving and assessing the reaction of fish to boats. I do not intend to repeat here what they have learnt but I can say that they can actually *feel* the approach of a boat with a petrol-burning outboard from over 100 yards and in several feet of water. I dread to think what the awareness of fish is to boats, with or without engines. I therefore think it wise to cut down movement and noise as much as is physically possible by the methods I have described.

Upton Broad was never easy and the bream and tench it contained were challenging fish. Things quickly changed for the worse as an extremely powerful corporation, whose angling club also had access, decided to pour in thousands of small roach, perch and carp. The fishing soon deteriorated and, although odd tench were boated, it was never to be the same again. The family at the farmhouse moved, the small fish bred and the matchmen descended. Upton died for me and I left the place for the last time feeling very sad.

Whenever I remember sitting in the sedge bank with the tench browsing in front of me or I hear the swish of the rod while I strike home the hook as a tench takes the bait on the shelf, a strong desire to return always haunts me. How I wish I could visit the past and enjoy those summer days again, afloat among the Upton tench!

and be ready to fish within minutes. It was just as well that I decided to leave the poles in as at the end of the campaign I was unable to remove them. A number of the sessions I spent fishing the shelf swim were quite blustery but the earlier effort and hassle of obtaining and inserting the poles was all worthwhile, since not a single bleep of the

Floats, Boats and Alderfen

Most of my own fishing for tench from boats has been with the float. The lift method was, and still is, a very productive and especially enjoyable way of capturing tench, even in these days of bolt rigs and boilies. There is a magic about the way that the quill dithers and rises out of the water to lie quivering in the surface film, before sliding away as the strike is made. But to use the method efficiently from a boat does take some practice.

There are two ways to fish the lift. I usually class these as 'correct' lift and 'tightened' lift. Correct lift is employed when the float is positioned away from the shot at the exact depth of the water. The line rising vertically can cause problems with false bites. For tightened lift the reel handle has to be turned slightly to cock the float so only the tip is visible as the float is set over depth.

Needless to say, this is very difficult from a boat and initially, with the rods resting across the gunwales, I struggled. With every movement the float would dip or rise. It wasn't until I began to use very long rod rests pushed into the mud *outside* the boat that the problem was solved completely and the lift method could be fished effectively and efficiently from the boat.

But, whether legering or float fishing, to fish afloat for tench during a warm, misty early-season dawn is to appreciate the epitome of boat fishing – the stillness of a flat calm so characteristic of summer, the tranquillity and remoteness, suddenly interrupted by frantic action and the arrival of a hard-fighting tench.

In the past I boat-fished for tench much more than I have done recently. In the late 1970s, Alderfen was my favourite location and the following tale tells the story of my first tench of a new season and the tactics that led to its downfall.

As I set out from the staging, aiming my boat in a bee-line for my chosen swim, the stillness seemed oppressive. Nothing broke the oily mirror-calm surface of the broad apart from the occasional early-morning insect or fry which dimpled in the reflection of a fast-fading moon. Mist hovered over the water as the cool morning air met the warm water and as I continued across the broad the rowlocks seemed to make a deafening noise. A fish bow-waved in front of me to my left, then another, and another – probably a shoal of bream moving and feeding across the shallow water, until I disturbed them.

I reached the swim I was intending to fish – a few yards of reed-fringed shoreline inaccessible from the bank, close to where a small bay met the main broad. Earlier reconnaissance here had revealed a small clump of bulrushes nestled in amongst the reeds. True to form, where these bulrushes had grown the bottom was a harder, gravelly contrast to the usual thick dark mud. The tench seemed to patrol along these marginal reeds, never remaining in one spot for any length of time but pausing to feed here and there. The close proximity to the reed corner formed by bay and broad seemed to be the ideal ambush spot to lure these patrolling tench.

A typically plump female tench is returned to the mirror-calm waters of the broad.

I halted the boat at one end of the swim and lowered the heavy double-headed boat rake silently over the side. Then, paying out the rake's cable, I rowed in a semicircle, avoiding the area to be fished, to where I met the reeds again at the other end of the swim. Here I pushed one of the mooring poles into the mud to anchor the boat at the bows and took up the slack cable to the rake.

Slowly I dragged the rake back, making sure that it worked a passage as close as possible to the edge of the reeds. One pull through was usually enough. I often wondered if this disturbance was scaring more tench than the rake attracted, but on previous occasions when I had arrived late and had tried without raking I usually went home fishless, and so, because it seemed that I owed most of my tench to the rake, I continued with the laborious procedure.

After clearing the rake of several old mussel shells and dead reeds, I repositioned the boat opposite the bulrushes about two rod lengths out. The next stage was to flick out several hookbait samples consisting of pieces of lobworm and flake, and to cast my two float-fished baits as close to the reeds as possible. I then settled back to blend gradually with the idyllic surroundings as the swim quietened down.

The first sign of activity was to my right. Out of the corner of my eye, I caught the movement of a section of reed stems as they began to quiver and shake, as if moved by an unseen hand. This reed shaking by the tench can be a real help where location is a problem. The daunting prospect of fishing a broad of many acres can be made relatively easy if you quietly drift along the reeds watching for the tell-tale signs.

A 'boat' rake, too large and heavy to be thrown, that has contributed to the capture of many tench.

Bubbles fizzed to the surface and small pieces of debris floated up, including some of my bread. I noticed a similar section of reeds doing likewise. The tench had obviously arrived.

The concentration on the two red-topped quills was intense. One flashed under and my hand hovered over the butt. The quill

A Broadland tench from amongst the bulrushes.

A big Alderfen tench is returned from one of the private jetties.

This large male tench swam around a mooring pole before obligingly untangling itself.

A recently spawned female taken on the lift method while boat fishing.

Early morning and a hefty tench is lifted aboard.

reappeared immediately – probably a line bite. More bubbles appeared round the other float and it began to twitch and gradually rose out of the water as the single swanshot was lifted from the bottom. A textbook lift bite, and I struck as the float lay flat. The rod arched over but I had contact for only a few seconds as a powerful tench ploughed into a thick outcrop of reeds on a short line and promptly deposited the hook securely amongst them.

I managed to free my line, and tranquillity returned to the broad as I waited for the tench to return, flicking in a few more hookbaits to encourage them. This short

lull in the activity was broken momentarily by a jack pike which picked up a half-lobworm but bit through the line shortly after the strike.

The tench then recommenced their barrage on the reeds. The next bite was as the first had been, a perfect lift bite, but this time I was ready for it. I struck as the float lay flat sending out tiny ripples. Even on a relatively short line I retained the upper hand, guiding the fish away from the sanctuary of the reeds out into the open water, finally netting it on the other side of the boat.

The long female had obviously spawned recently and pulled the scales down to five pounds five ounces. But I was well pleased with my first tench from the broad that season – and a five pounder at that!

I managed to enlist the help of an angler just setting up to take some photographs for me; then, after measuring the fish, I leaned over the side of the boat and gently lowered her back into the water.

I fished on until about 7.30 a.m. but had no other bites. The tench could probably have been lured back into the swim but I couldn't afford to be late for work again. One pricked fish and another boated would probably keep them down for quite a while, especially in the crystal-clear water. And so, with the warm glow of success and the early morning sun, I packed up and rowed back, already eagerly anticipating the evening session.

Three Francis Francis punts unloading after a day on the river.   (Photo: Bill Rushmer)

Room within the close confines of a boat is always at a premium.

In an idyllic setting, Eric Barnes returns a large bream from the punt. (Photo: Graham Marsden)

A tranquil scene at the end of the bream fisher's day. (Photo: Graham Marsden)

A fantastic 17lb 11oz fully scaled mirror for John Webb, captured with the assistance of an inflatable dinghy. (Photo: John Webb)

Baiting up for carp from an inflatable as dusk closes in. (Photo: John Webb)

Bev's first from the Horseshoe Lake, an immaculate 16lb 5oz. (Photo: John Webb)

Nick Beardmore poses with a 6lb tench.   (Photo: Roger Miller)

Roger Miller with a large Upton tench from the 'Shelf'.   (Photo: Roger Miller)

Boat fishing for rudd on Annaghmore Lough, Ireland. (Photo: Kevin Clifford)

Kevin Clifford poses with a shared catch of rudd of over 100lb taken from a boat on Annaghmore Lough. (Photo: Kevin Clifford)

Pete Rogers with a superb perch of 3lb 10oz. (Photo: Pete Rogers)

Dressed for protection against the weather, Pete Rogers returns another big Bewl perch. (Photo: Pete Rogers)

In windless conditions, Stephen Harper battles against a Lomond Pike.

A 22lb 6oz River Bure pike that fell to a float paternostered live roach.

A Norfolk pike of 26lb 10oz from a tidal river, held in the close confines of the author's small dinghy.

On a still, winter's day, a small pike is boated by hand. (Photo: Dave Humphries)

Gord Burton displays a 23lb 10oz pike that fell to a tadpolly plug. (Photo: Gord Burton)

Mike Saunt displays the unusual two-tone variation on a small pike.

A lone angler against the backdrop of the glens. (Photo: Kevin Maxfield)

Winter weather on the loch. (Photo: Gord Burton)

Stephen Harper with a summer-caught 23 pounder from Loch Lomond.

The American way: baseball hat, bright jacket, padded swivel chair and a bass on a lure. (Photo: Martyn Page)

Getting to the swim American style – with a 35 hp outboard!

A catch of large mouthed bass, walleye and 'northerns' from Canada's Lake Despair.

Reward for a day on Lake Michigan. Two big salmon on stringers. (Photo: Martyn Page)

Afloat in Pursuit of Roach and Rudd

by Kevin Clifford

Kevin Clifford is renowned for the capture of many very large fish of a wide variety of species and the innovative thinking that has helped put them on the bank. He has a great knowledge of all aspects of angling and a special affection for carp fishing is reflected in a deep interest in the history of that branch of the sport. Kevin is at present working on a book which will detail this fascinating subject. His first book, Redmire Pool, *co-authored with Len Arbury, was published in 1984. He has also contributed to several other angling books and writes regularly for the angling monthlies.*

A member of the Yorkshire Fisheries Consultative Association and of numerous other committees, Kevin works hard for angling and is a strong supporter of the National Association of Specialist Anglers and the Anglers' Co-operative Association, believing that all anglers should give their support to such bodies to safeguard the future of our sport for the generations to come.

Kevin's contribution gives an interesting insight into tackling roach and rudd fishing from afloat. These two species are possibly the most easily frightened of all fish where boats are concerned and call for stealth and caution. But, once located, Kevin has found that they are not so difficult to catch.

SH

Without doubt, boat fishing can offer substantial advantages over bank fishing, and sometimes disadvantages. Certain fish, such as pike and perch, appear at times to be attracted to boats, whilst other fish such as roach and rudd are easily disturbed by the presence of boats and great care is required not to alarm the fish, particularly in shallow water. It is usually on the larger waters that boat fishing provides the most benefits, although even on the smallest of fisheries a boat can sometimes be indispensable. Fish have a habit of seeking out those areas which are inaccessible to the bank fisher. Occasionally bank fishing is difficult, sometimes downright impossible, and very often on large waters the fish don't come near the banks anyway. Two classic examples of this are Hornsea Mere in Yorkshire and Annaghmore Lough just outside Strokestown in Ireland. Hornsea Mere is over 400 acres of shallow water, with a maximum depth of about six feet. It has a dense marginal cover of Norfolk reed, some ten to twenty feet wide, and offers very little bank fishing. The water is very shallow in the margins and the large roach tend to stay well out from the bank in deeper water.

The question of location is always the main key to success on these large waters and as long as the fish can be approached without disturbance they tend to be fairly easy to catch. Sometimes, unconventional yet obvious approaches can be successful. On Hornsea Mere, location is absolutely vital. About one-third of the mere is a bird sanctuary and out of bounds for fishing and boating. It is likely that many of the fish spend much of their time in these areas. Time and again it has been shown that random fishing at various spots round the mere is invariably a complete waste of time. Weekend fishing is difficult during the summer months as the fishing has to be shared with other water users whose activities have an adverse effect. The most successful method of location seems to be to spend a considerable amount of time rowing slowly around the mere, in mid-week, in weather conditions which reduce the numbers of other water users, looking until coloured water and/or signs of feeding fish are found. Many trips may prove uneventful, but when a shoal of feeding roach is finally found the resulting catches can be exceptional. Ideally, it requires one person to stand in the bow of the boat using binoculars and, if necessary, polarising glasses, with another person rowing. If I had to choose one particular time of day to locate roach it would be the last hour before dark, especially on those warm, still, muggy, sometimes drizzly evenings. At such times big roach show themselves by priming on the surface and this rolling is always associated with feeding. Find priming roach and you are more than halfway to catching them.

The sixty-acre Annaghmore Lough also has shallow margins with large beds of Norfolk reed and bulrush growing in profusion. The rudd do come into very shallow water close to, or actually in the reed beds in warm sunny weather but generally, because it seems to me the sun doesn't shine much in Ireland, they are not far from deeper water; this is often on the side of the reed beds facing towards the centre of the lake. In these circumstances they are best approached from a boat so that hooked fish can be drawn away from the shoal into the reed-clear deeper water. Trying to catch these fish from the bank would normally necessitate trying to pull them through the reed beds in very shallow water, causing tremendous disturbance. With a pair of binoculars in sunny, windless conditions rudd will sooner or later betray their presence. A shoal of large rudd, their backs just dimpling the surface, can be passed over as the action of small fry. But keep watching, and when they are disturbed by a bird flying over watch the water explode as they scatter.

Boat fishing, particularly on large feature-less meres and lakes, is not ordinarily undertaken by the average angler. Frankly, at times it can be soul-destroying. Sitting in the uncomfortable conditions of a 10-foot boat on a 400-acre lake a few miles from the North Sea in the middle of winter, with a brisk north-easterly coming straight from the Russian steppes, is not for the faint-hearted. In addition, many anglers find rowing difficult and good boat handling is an acquired skill, coming only with practice. The bonus is that, because these difficulties tend to keep a great many anglers from fishing such waters, the fish are hardly ever caught. Fish which are rarely fished for are, once located, easy to catch. It has been said by several eminent anglers in the past that fish which live in rich waters with ample supplies of natural food and are not often fished for are difficult to catch. I must say that my experience suggests the opposite. Such fish demand simple baits and methods. Fancy rigs and complex baits are, by and large, not required. Unless fishing in very shallow water for rudd, less than a couple of feet or so, when a basic sliding link leger or paternoster is ideal, a straightforward antenna-type float covers the majority of fishing situations. A good-sized float will be necessary to cast a reasonable distance and to carry enough lead to hold in position.

Len Head displays a large haul of rudd from Annaghmore Lough.
                    Photo: Kevin Clifford

Even with light winds, big expanses of water have powerful undertows.

The majority of the big roach and rudd that I have caught whilst boat fishing have fallen to a handful of simple baits – bread flake, sweetcorn, bread crust, maggots and worms, with flake and corn as my first choice. However, it doesn't pay to be too dogmatic about baits. The large roach of Hornsea Mere are invariably caught only on large worms. This was so during the big roach bonanza at Hornsea during the early part of this century and, most strangely, it is still the case today.

But whether the quarry is roach or rudd on mere, lough or lake, the advantages of using a boat on these larger waters are obvious and increase the angler's chance of success many times over.

Lake Rudd and River Roach

by John Bailey

John Bailey is reknowned throughout the angling world as a successful angler and author. During a long angling career he has pursued and captured many large fish of most of the freshwater species, but is perhaps best known as an expert on roach and rudd.

He is a prolific angling writer and has written many books, including In Visible Waters, Travels with a Two Piece, Reflections from the Water's Edge *and* Roach – The Gentle Giants, *and has co-authored books on pike, carp and bream with Martyn Page and Roger Miller, both also contributors to this book. Besides books, John also writes regularly for weekly and monthly angling publications when his fishing permits. At present, he is deeply concerned with environmental issues and is especially involved in the problems of our declining upper rivers.*

SH

Today in 1989, the majority of my fishing is geared towards the major predators of the United Kingdom, pike and the great cannibal brown trout, the so-called ferox of Scotland. After neither of these species do I feel confident unless I have a boat available. My approach from bank alone I will always believe inadequate, and as a result I fish with little conviction and generally with even less success.

Now, if we go back ten years when roach and rudd were probably my favourite quarry, the same was true. Even if I did not always pursue them from a boat, I always liked one to hand for a wide variety of purposes. Looking back into my memory and my records, I have no doubt that the ability to get on the water often caught me bonus fish.

A boat had its most obvious uses on stillwaters – whether large pits, broads or even the estate lakes which gave me so many fabulous rudd a decade ago. The important thing to remember, with rudd especially, is that they hardly ever patrol the easily fishable banks of a water. Big rudd are exceptionally sensitive to disturbance and the chances of ambush close in, during the daylight hours at least, are slight. Long casting or preferably getting afloat are vital.

LAKE RUDD

Rudd spend the majority of the daylight hours either in the central areas of a water, as far as possible from any bank, or holed up in areas that they have come to regard as sanctuaries. When in sanctuary they are easier to get at and to catch! The places to look for are in the fringes of inaccessible weed and reed beds, around far sides of islands, under remote beds of lilies and particularly in amongst the branches of fallen trees. In short, any area that sees little disturbance and few baits is worth investigation.

I presume that the bulk of most anglers' rudd fishing will be done in the summer, when the probability of fish showing themselves on the surface is high. Therefore take binoculars afloat, so that you can see the shoals long before the boat disturbs them. Scan the sanctuary areas constantly from a good way out and, once rudd are spotted, plan the approach.

Above all, come up close to a rudd shoal with the greatest possible caution. Do not think of using an outboard – not even an electric one. Row very slowly, carefully and quietly. Personally, I do not believe it is overdoing the caution even to muffle the oars. Anchor up as far away as casting allows and try, if at all possible, to have the wind at your back. I say this for a very important reason: my first approach will always be with floating baits, and with the wind behind me I can drift free offerings into the sanctuary area without spooking the shoal in any way. The traditional favourite floating bait for rudd has always been bread crust and this, of course, is still efficient today. My favourites, however, are well-soaked Chum Mixer biscuits stolen from my dog's bowl. They can be placed for thirty seconds or so in plain boiling water to make them soft enough for the hook, and one of the many carp flavourings can be added. Anything sweet, maple in particular, will catch rudd.

Position the boat thirty or forty yards from the topping rudd – aren't those vivid red fins a glorious sight in the sunlight? – and drift the Chum over to the area. Do not despair if the first few offerings are not accepted. It might take ten or fifteen minutes and a good hundred biscuits before the rudd show interest, but they surely will in the end and then the excitement is heart stopping.

Use a light 11- to 13-foot rod and 3- or 4-pound line, well greased, straight through to a size 10 hook with a biscuit sitting on the shank. For casting weight, a small bubble float filled with the necessary amount of water cannot really be bettered. Aim to drop your own bait some five yards short of the taking area and let it make its own way on the breeze into the fish. Watch the bubble float and strike as it moves off, or, better still, watch your bait through the binoculars. I find it truly exciting to see the white lips take the bait and the line skid along after the turning fish. Once hooked, bully the fish quickly from the area. A shoal will not take too much disturbance and after a few fish have been caught you will find it breaking up and moving to new areas of so-called safety.

More difficult to catch are the rudd that spend the day drifting in open water. These fish are more difficult to approach than the sanctuary rudd and, worse still, they rarely remain static but seem constantly to follow the breezes. I can only suggest that your boat does the same thing. Let it drift, do not use the oars more than necessary and keep a constant look-out for rudd coming into casting range. I use a long light rod loaded with 2- to 6-pound line and a heavy self-locking float. Under this, I tie a size 8 hook baited with a large knob of bread flake. This rig can be cast a good fifty yards and as soon as I see fish within that range, out it goes. Takes are nearly always instant – though often the shoal will move before giving you a second chance. Frequently, I have spent all day on the drift and only made a dozen or so casts. However, if these account for rudd averaging a pound or so I make no complaint.

STILLWATER ROACH

Boat fishing for roach on stillwaters I generally reserve for the winter. As temperatures fall, roach tend to move into the deepest holes and gullies on large pits and there they stay unless the weather becomes very mild, wet and windy. Often, these deep areas are close enough to the bank to be fished easily but, even when they are, after a few roach have been taken the shoal often moves further

John Bailey admires a boat-caught estate-lake rudd.

out to more distant deeps. This is when the boat is again vital.

With modern echo-sounders and even better, fish finders, a few hours on the biggest pit will give you the best possible locations. Once the roach are found, you can go at them with the utmost confidence. Even now, though, there are pitfalls and a definite battle plan should be followed.

Rather unlike winter pike fishing, roach fishing calls for great finesse and tackle control. With low temperatures, I suggest it is impossible to fish effectively all day long and only the best times should be attempted. In my opinion, it is good to get out at first light and fish till, say, 9 or 10 a.m., or better still to start in the mid-afternoon and fish on till dusk. If you concentrate on short two- or three-hour sessions, the cold is not too

great a problem and you can fish effectively over roach you are sure are present.

Pits are rarely calm in winter and the boat needs to be very securely anchored. I choose to have the wind behind me and I moor on the shallows immediately upwind, fishing down into the deeps. I do not like an umbrella in a boat, but prefer to wear one of the modern one-piece fishing suits. Even in rain and sleet, with my back to the wind, I can fish for roach as snug as anything with full control and concentration.

As to actual methods, I float-fish exactly as I would on the bank, only now far more convinced that I am actually on roach rather than empty water.

RIVER ROACH

Over the years boats have proved very useful for my river roaching. I do not often use them to fish from, but rather to find roach in the first place. Now that the rivers have such low stocks of fish, the importance of this facility cannot be overrated. In the summer of 1985 I was contemplating a September campaign after roach on a very clear upper river but I was not at all sure that any real numbers of fish remained. I walked the banks but saw nothing, so luxuriant was the weed. I knew I needed to be *on* the water rather than *beside* it. As a result, on a bright, late August morning I pushed myself off in a light ten-foot boat from below one of the mills. I had a couple of paddles, a loaf of bread, polaroid glasses, anchor and rope and several plastic-bottle marker buoys tied to corks and weights. Off I set, not rowing exactly but rather going with the current and directing myself with the paddle if I wanted to investigate some feature. On the summer flow I moved very slowly and gently and I was able to observe virtually the whole river. The boat glided so serenely that to the fish it merely resembled floating debris. Within 200 yards I was able to get right over the top of a shoal of chub and feed them with scraps of flake.

On two occasions along my four-mile journey I actually saw roach, big ones, and popped out the marker buoys to guide me later in the day when I would walk the stretch. Far more often, however, I discovered deeper holes, where the bed had been scraped clear of algae, possibly by bottom-feeding fish. These areas too were marked and later investigated from the bank.

The day proved to be a success. Seeing the fish made me realise that roach were still present and worth trying for; seeing possible feeding areas gave me valuable pointers to swims. Indeed, some six or seven weeks later, as darkness fell, I fished one of the marked areas and landed an excellent roach of nearly three pounds. Without that boat trip I really doubt if I would ever have mounted the campaign at all.

On larger roach rivers such as the Wye, the Tweed, the Thames or the tidal Yare, I can see real advantages in boat and fish-finder work. Choosing winter swims is always difficult but, if a stretch can be covered by boat and if fish can actually be found, then success becomes immediately obtainable. There are those who would question the ethics of such a high-tech approach, but I cannot really agree with them. Science has given roach anglers a really useful tool in the fish finder and it is blind not to use it in certain locations. Indeed, now that river roach are ever more rare these aids do little more than redress the balance that was rapidly tipping against us, the anglers. By all means, fish for roach and rudd traditionally from the bank, but my belief is that your results will be the poorer for it. Stay open-minded, become adaptable and above all, get afloat!

Reservoir Perch

by Stuart Allum with Pete Rogers

Stuart Allum is Secretary of the Perchfishers but his interests are in no way restricted to one species. A member of the Chub Study Group and the National Association of Specialist Anglers, he has taken specimens of chub, pike, barbel, roach and tench along with perch to three pounds eight and a half ounces. A confirmed all-rounder, he is just as happy fly-fishing for trout, legering a worm for perch or trolling for some strange and exotic species on occasional trips abroad.

Pete Rogers is the motivating force behind the reformation of the Perchfishers. He is an avid collector of angling books and periodicals and has collated almost everything written on perch fishing over the last one hundred years, including the details of all perch in excess of three pounds reported to the angling press since records began (almost three thousand individual captures). Quite naturally, therefore, he has taken on the role as records officer for the Perchfishers.

Another all-rounder, Pete enjoys barbel fishing on the middle Avon in Hampshire and also pursues pike, tench, roach and rudd. His best perch to date is a terrific boat-caught fish of three pounds ten ounces.

Stuart and Pete describe graphically the way in which they go about tackling the large reservoirs of southern England in search of that most beautiful of freshwater fish, the perch.

SH

My own experience of boat fishing for perch began when some of the large trout reservoirs in the south of England, notably Bewl Bridge reservoir, were opened during the autumn months for pike fishing after the trout season had ended.

My friends and I quickly discovered that the perch-fishing potential of these huge, clean and fertile waters easily equalled, and in some cases surpassed, that of the pike fishing. The pike, after all, is a fish which is best suited to a low-density population environment. When these reservoirs were opened the pike soon came under intense pressure from some of the country's keenest pike anglers – hardly surprising when a great many of these hitherto uncaught fish were prime specimens in the twenty- to thirty-pound bracket. After only a couple of seasons a large proportion of these great fish had been caught and, sadly, due to the philistine fishery regulations in force, removed. The result was that these reservoirs soon became overpopulated with hundreds of tiny pike in the two- to five-pound bracket, with doubles a comparative rarity. This also appears to be true of other waters which have suffered a similar fate.

This situation, however, does not apply to the perch. Provided they have a suitable environment, perch are capable of happily co-existing in massive shoals holding hundreds of fish, all of specimen size. It was therefore far more appealing to fish for the perch, where a bag of fish in the two- to three-pound bracket was quite possible, than to try in vain for one of the remaining outsize pike, only to be rewarded with an endless succession of jacks.

TIME OF YEAR

The autumn months, from late September through to early December, are by far the best months of the year for catching quality perch in any numbers. Temperatures are usually fairly high (in the mid-50s) and conditions often remain calm and settled for weeks on end. However, a slow but inevitable decline in temperatures occurs throughout this period and this has a marked effect on the behaviour patterns of the perch. Fish which were widespread and difficult to pin down during the summer months now begin to shoal up in vast numbers, heading for the deeper areas of the lake. The larger fish are particularly active at this time of year and may often be encountered in large shoals. When this occurs and the angler has positioned himself correctly, sport can be fast and furious and of unbelievable quality. As the winter months progress and temperatures decline still further, perch activity slows down almost to a standstill and, whilst the fish may still be located (usually in very deep water), their feeding periods are generally much shorter, with the bigger fish becoming very hard to entice. With the onset of warmer weather, usually in early March, the fish again become active and this is often the time when some of the very largest perch are caught. However, weather conditions at this time of year are often very unsettled, and the occasions when boat fishing is possible exceedingly limited before the season closes.

WEATHER CONDITIONS

The perch is by nature a sight feeder and therefore is obviously going to be most active during the daylight hours. During the autumn months the better fish are usually located in depths of twenty feet or more where light penetration is low, even on the brightest days. However, the perch has very keen eyesight, and even low light values are enough for it to become extremely active. Indeed, some of my best catches have been made on very dull, choppy days and in heavy rain. The fact of the matter is that so long as the water is not too cold perch will feed during the daylight hours whatever the light penetration.

Perhaps my favourite weather conditions of all are those days when a light south-westerly breeze just ruffles the surface and the sun shines intermittently from behind light cloud cover. These settled conditions, in which temperatures remain unaltered for long periods, often encourage heavy feeding amongst the larger perch, with fish remaining active in the same area for weeks on end.

Flat calm conditions with brilliant sunshine are, as with most species, very poor for perch fishing, despite their being sight feeders. On these days, however, the dawn and dusk periods can sometimes provide very good sport and a spinner slowly retrieved beneath the fiery glow of an autumnal sunset is often too much for the perch, deep below and gazing upwards, to resist.

The only conditions which I suggest you avoid are those days when a chilling east wind whips across the surface, sending both air and water temperatures plummeting. These conditions are uncomfortable for both angler and fish and it is unlikely that a responsible fishery manager would allow you to venture very far in a boat in any case. Similarly, those days immediately following a heavy storm may provide poor sport as the sudden influx of cold, dirty water from

The best of six fish all over 2 pounds, a 2lb 10oz perch taken in very windy conditions. A life-jacket is always a wise precaution.

Photo: Stuart Allum

swollen feeder streams often puts the fish down for a while. The weeks immediately following the hurricane of October 1987 were a prime example, and perch sport on the larger reservoirs (Ardleigh, for example) declined drastically until conditions became more settled. This statement should not be taken as a contradiction of what I said earlier about stormy weather. The fishing *during* a heavy rainstorm can often be quite superb, provided of course that conditions are not so windy as to prevent safe boat handling.

LOCATION

As mentioned earlier, the fish at this time of year will be in tightly packed shoals migrating into deeper water as the conditions become colder. This migration is a slow process, as the perch is constructed in such a way that delicate adjustments in its swim bladder need to be made each time a significant change in depth is necessitated. It therefore follows that, provided temperatures remain settled, fish may be found at the same depth for weeks on end until a drop in temperature forces them deeper. As a general rule of thumb, however, I would look for those areas where there is a sudden drop-off from shallow water to a depth of about twenty-five feet, especially where there is some cover nearby (trout cages, moored boats and the like). These places are excellent spots to try during the early autumn months and may be found only thirty yards or so offshore on 'natural' reservoirs (flooded valleys). By December, though, the fish may well have moved into the very deepest water they can find, way out in the centre of

The dorsal fin of this 2lb 7½oz Bewl Bridge perch is displayed by its captor Nigel Witham.
Photo: Stuart Allum

the reservoir and in depths of up to fifty or even sixty feet.

Hot spots can be located in a number of ways. I personally favour the study of bank-side features. A steeply shelving bank with deep water close to the shoreline is an obvious place to try, whereas a gently shelving bank leading into extensive shallows where the water, accentuated by wave action, creates a considerable undertow does not generally offer much in the way of perch fishing. Dams and valve towers are other obvious places to try as there is nearly always deep water nearby, and often large shoals of roach fry. This is another important factor, as the perch will never be far from their food source. At Ardleigh reservoir the bank sides at weekends are often crowded with match fishermen, and if your venue is of a similar nature keep an eye on those areas which are producing the best roach fishing. The perch will usually be encountered further out in deeper water on the periphery of the roach shoals.

The use of electronic fish finders and echo-sounders is now widespread amongst pike anglers on our larger waters and can be equally useful for perch location. Fellow Perchfishers Pete Rogers and Steve Burke have used these devices to good effect on a number of occasions and they are particularly useful on the more 'featureless' areas of water, where bank-side features give no clue to the lake-bed contours, say, 100 yards offshore. Underwater currents sometimes create deep depressions in the bed of a reservoir and these are prime holding areas, yet they would go unnoticed but for the use of an echo-sounder. Steve Burke found such a hot spot on Bewl Bridge some years ago and took ten perch, all in the two- to three-pound range, during an afternoon session from an area we had all passed over without realising its potential.

So there you have it. Whilst there is no substitute for watercraft, there is a place for both natural experience and instinct, and the use of modern technology in the location of fish and fish-holding areas on these vast expanses of water where a boat is essential.

Lastly, if you locate a possible hot spot in deep water yet draw a blank there, do not discount the area altogether. Remember that as the perch migrate to deeper water they will often move considerable distances to find a comfortable spot at the right depth and an area which was devoid of fish one week may be teeming with them the next.

METHODS

Spinning

My favourite method by far, and one which is capable of sorting out large fish in good numbers when applied properly, is spinning. Remember that the fish you are seeking will be in deep water and that a spoon which can hold its depth for a long period during a slow retrieve will work best of all. By far the best lure invented for this type of work is the Abu Atom. With its convex shape and slow, fluttering action, this lure has outscored all others by far for consistent perch success. The slowest retrieve is sufficient for water pressure underneath the Atom's curved surface to hold it just clear of the bottom and it will maintain its action right to the surface. Indeed, perch will sometimes follow this lure right up through thirty feet of water and take it right underneath the boat. Other good patterns include the Abu Toby and some of the large copper spoons now available for pike fishing. The Professor range, recently imported from America, also has a strong perch-killing reputation, though I have yet to try this pattern myself.

Do not be afraid to use the largest patterns you can find. A big perch will easily engulf a 4-inch or 5-inch spoon and I have caught really tiny perch which I have had difficulty in removing from a lure much larger than themselves. They really are most aggressive fish, and will not be deterred from attacking the largest prey once they have made up their minds to do so. Indeed, the additional weight of the larger lures makes them easier to control at long range and in deep water, thus adding to their effectiveness. They are also, of course, much more easily visible to the perch, lying down there in the darkness. Colour is really a matter of personal choice, but gold, silver, copper and 'perch' patterns have all yielded good catches, with gold and 'perch' patterns generally the most consistent overall.

An Abu Atom secured the downfall of this perfect 2 pounder.
Photo: Stuart Allum

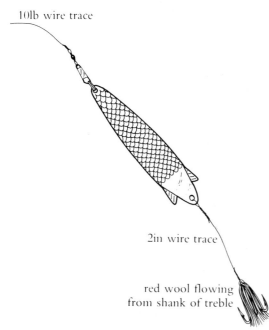

10lb wire trace

2in wire trace

red wool flowing
from shank of treble

Fig 22 'Flyer' spoon rig.

Remember that a perch usually attacks its prey from behind, snapping at its tail in order to cripple it before engulfing it. Very often, whilst spinning, the angler will feel a series of knocks on the rod top before encountering a solid take. Do not strike at these tappings and do not slow the retrieve or stop winding; merely continue retrieving at a steady pace or even slightly faster. There will be no mistaking the solid weight of a well-hooked perch when it eventually takes the lure.

In order to encourage pursuing fish to take a lure, I usually adorn the treble hook with red wool, or sometimes add a similarly adorned 'flyer' hook a couple of inches behind the lure so as to imitate the enticing tail of a small fish *(see* Fig. 22). Perch do have a keen sense of smell and dipping the wool in a fish-flavoured solution is also worth trying.

I normally use a wire trace because of the inevitable presence of pike, and this does not deter the perch at all. Whilst I normally use a fine nylon-covered or 'pikestrand' trace of no more than 10- to 15-pound BS, my colleague Pete Rogers uses 20-pound traces for trolling work and has found that they make no difference.

Tackle for Spinning

For spinning, the rod must be able to complement the action of the lure without impairing it. My personal choice is an old Bruce & Walker MK 4 compound-taper 10 footer, which shows every movement of the lure in its soft tip section yet has plenty of power in the middle and butt for striking and playing fish. Far too many so-called spinning rods have no action at all and merely bend into one continuous arc on the retrieve. This unexciting characteristic can greatly impair the effectiveness of the lure. The crux of the matter is properly balanced tackle. Remember that you are trying to imitate the action of a small live fish in distress and not simply pulling a lump of metal through the water, so choose a rod that has a supple, sensitive tip yet sufficient power in its lower sections to enable you to fish at long range in deep water. For this reason, you may find that a lighter fibreglass model has some advantages over certain carbon rods, so choose carefully.

Lines for spinning would ideally be in the 6- to 8-pound range, matched to a rod in the 1¼- to 1½-pound test-curve bracket. I favour Maxima, which is a good performer where the line is continually being punished by repeated casting and retrieving. The breaking strain is rather crucial. Anything below 6-pound BS is bound to suffer and weaken as a result of the excessive punishment caused by continually punching out lures weighing 1 ounce or more, whilst a line of over 8-pound BS is too thick and heavy, will impair casting and create too much drag in the water, spoiling the action of the lure.

Worm Fishing

It is strange that on some waters spinning will work best yet on others will hardly raise a take, whilst the perch will attack worms in almost suicidal fashion. The preferences of the fish vary from water to water and where they prefer bait there is no doubt that the worm is by far their favourite. My preference with this method is to find some cover (for example a trout cage or some other feature such as a buoy), ground-bait little and often with maggots to attract small roach and perch into the vicinity, then fish a worm close to the bottom in the hope of a bigger fish. The activity of all the small fish usually attracts the larger perch into the area. The only problem in catching them is that they are usually heavily outnumbered by their smaller brethren, who are also irresistibly attracted by worms. This is a cross you will just have to bear, and it is for this reason that I always try to amass a large supply of lobworms (up to 100 if possible) before a trip. They don't last very long.

I always try to get the worm to behave as naturally as possible and therefore prefer a slowish descent rather than a fast one. For this reason I use a barrel or coffin lead (see Fig. 23), which, being long in section, tends to sink in a slow arc, rather than an Arlesey bomb, which plunges straight to the bottom. My usual rig is simply an Avon rod, 4- or 5-pound line and a ¼-ounce coffin or barrel lead stopped about 30 inches from a size 6 or 8 hook baited with a whole lobworm. Kirby hooks (see Fig. 24), old-fashioned though they may be, are ideal for this type of fishing as the tiny barbs on the shank help to secure the worm but cause no damage to the perch.

Bites are easily registered on the rod tip but I prefer to touch leger, with my index finger trapping the line against the edge of the open reel spool. That way I can release line to a taking fish and offer minimal resis-

tance. Perch hate resistance. There is no need to strike too hard. You are generally right above the fish in a boat, and all that is needed is to engage the pick-up gently and raise the rod while winding in rapidly. This will result in more fish hooked against a tight line than striking hard against thirty feet of water and an unknown amount of slack line.

Lastly, if a bite is not forthcoming after a reasonable period of time, don't just leave the bait on the bottom and expect the perch to find it. Perch are aggressive fish and a moving bait will usually attract them. I

Stuart Allum with a medium-sized Bewl Bridge fish.

Photo: Stuart Allum

Diagram (a) shows the more natural, slow-sinking arc created by a coffin or barrel lead as opposed to the Arlesy bomb shown in (b), which sinks fast and straight down, the worm behind it. The arc in (a) covers a far greater area and is therefore effective longer.

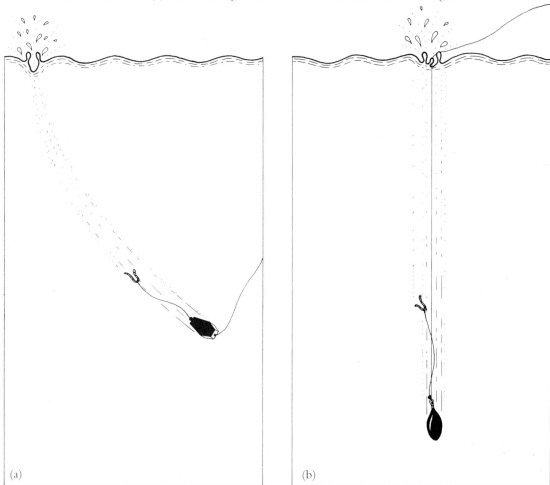

(a)

(b)

Fig 23   (a) Coffin or barrel lead   (b) Arlesey bomb.

always try to keep the worm on the move by jigging it up and down, sometimes winding in a few feet and letting the worm sink down again. It is surprising how many takes occur immediately after a bait has been moved, often when it is several feet clear of the bottom.

Livebaiting

This is another good method for sorting out the better fish, especially where the use of worms is hindered by the presence of too many small perch. Again, however, I like to keep plenty of small fish in the area by loose-feeding maggots. The rig usually consists of a sliding float paternoster with the bait set to fish about three feet off the bottom. It is, of course, necessary to use a wire trace because of the presence of pike, but here, unlike in spinning, it is important to use as fine a wire trace as possible, as a big perch will have much more time to inspect the bait at close quarters before deciding

Small barbs
on shank help
to secure a large,
lively lobworm

Fig 24 *'Kirby'-type hook.*

whether to attack. By far the best choice of bait is in fact a small perch four to five inches long. The strike should be made as soon as possible before the perch drops the bait, which it is likely to do as soon as it feels the resistance unavoidably caused by the pater-noster lead.

TROLLING
by Pete Rogers

Rods for Trolling

As previously mentioned by Stewart, I also believe that a quality glass-fibre rod cannot be bettered in many aspects. In my experience the current ultra-modern materials very often equate to an inherently stiff rod lacking the general sensitivity and feel to be found in the medium of glass, and I therefore feel that we should seek to combine the merits of both to produce the best tool for what is sometimes a surprisingly shy-biting species.

My present set-up consists of a 9-foot parabolic carbon-glass composite blank with a Duplon-covered crank handle for multiplier use. As my perch fishing is carried out during the winter months the warm feel

and lack of slipperiness of Duplon is clearly an asset. The choice of rod fitments is also important and the use of Fuji aluminium oxide or silicone carbide rings is essential on any rod intended for trolling. If a lot of use is to be made of the rod I would suggest that you opt for double-footed rings, which are more robust and will stand up to rougher treatment. My own preference, however, is for single-leg spinning rings, which do not spoil the action of the rod, though of course they are more fragile.

This light, well-balanced rod can be hand-held *all day,* which is another important factor. Unless you can get hold of a propri-etary American rod rest specifically intended for trolling (or make your own) my advice is to forget it. The boat rod rests sold in this country are meant to hold the rod whilst the craft is stationary and very little more than that. I would certainly never risk a valuable rod and reel balanced precariously over the side on one of these flimsy contraptions at anything like a fast trolling speed. In any case, by holding the rod at all times and feeling for bites I am totally confident of catching more fish than the lazy angler who simply waits for a fish to hang itself.

Reels, Lines and Traces

I favour a relatively small left-hand-wind multiplier and the Abu XLT FL LH fits the bill nicely. Being of polycarbonate con-struction, it is both light and durable, holds more than sufficient line for trolling purposes and has the benefit of relatively high gearing. The XLT also has the advantages of flipping trigger and thumb bar. This allows you to pay out line at will by depressing the thumb bar, without having to disconnect the drive mechanism. Anyone who has done any trolling with biggish lures will know of the difficulty which can be encountered in trying to disengage the spool to release line when the rod and reel are under extreme tension, and this little gadget does away with the problem altogether.

As far as lines are concerned, I normally opt for a line of 11- to 12-pound BS and can recommend both Maxima and Sylcast. You will note that this is stronger than Stewart has recommended for spinning, but trolling subjects the line to much greater impact (from hooked fish) and stretching. Also, the possibility of hooking into large pike has to be taken into consideration as trolling is also very effective for them. In the near future I intend to experiment much more with pre-stretched lines, particularly braided nylon, to see if my catch rate improves. Imagine the stretch in, say, fifty or sixty yards of normal 12-pound BS monofilament.

As Stewart has already mentioned, I use a fairly heavy trace of 20-pound BS for all my plug-trolling sessions. These are the short 8-inch black-nylon-covered wire spinning traces manufactured by Berkeley. This may seem disproportionately strong but the merit of the 8-inch trace is its resistance to kinking, the attention it gets from pikes' teeth and the large American snap swivel with which it is fitted. This last point is most important. Whichever trace you opt for, make sure it allows your lure *maximum* mobility and is strong. For spoons and spinners I use a longer trace of up to 24 inches incorporating a ball-bearing swivel, which slows down the process of line twist but does not eradicate it completely.

Lures for Trolling

A whole book could be written on the subject of lure selection alone. My advice is to read all the current American material on the subject you can find. From my own experience, however, I would urge you to think big when seeking large perch and use a lure with plenty of action or vibration. By large, I do not mean ludicrously so but my first choice of lure is about 5 inches long.

Colour seems to be a critical factor and silver-plated plugs in the Helin Flatfish range have worked wonders for me when identical lures in different colour patterns have been ignored. Nevertheless, do not be afraid to experiment and never be too dogmatic in your approach.

Do not forget that your perch may be in as much as thirty feet of water, so bear this in mind and choose a lure which is capable of working at such depths.

Preparation

Perhaps the two most important elements in any trolling situation are boat control and lure presentation. The first can only be gained by experience, by putting in time on the water under every variation of season and weather conditions. Watch an angler familiar with trolling and it looks easy, a piece of cake. He will very gently control and correct his course without any noticeable effort or thought to achieve the trolling run he requires. Try it yourself and you will very quickly realise just how difficult it is to become proficient in this style of fishing. If you don't agree, then look at the stern of your boat and I can almost guarantee it will have left a zigzag pattern in the water showing your wandering course, despite all efforts to keep a straight line. Slow the boat down to a very slow trolling speed in a stiff breeze and the problems are magnified.

Concentration is important, of course, but other small factors can also make a difference between success or failure. Remember that it is not the boat that you are trying to place over the fish but your lure, which may be anything up to sixty yards astern.

First make sure that the person controlling the boat has a comfortable seating position and some foam padding or something similar to sit on. I also suggest that you slightly offset the motor to give a more comfortable grip on the throttle. Similarly, the position of any electronic aid (fish finder or echo-sounder) is also crucial; it must be easily viewed by the operator under varying light conditions. Lack of attention to these points can result in severe discomfort or backache, which will soon lead to erratic and inefficient boat performance.

Secondly, pare down your equipment until you have the absolute minimum necessary on board. Too much clutter in the boat only gets in the way, and loose lures can be a confounded nuisance, and danger-ous, if a big fish is brought aboard.

Thirdly, plan ahead. If you intend to fish a trout reservoir during the winter months, take a boat round during the spring or summer for a recce. Make up a map or, better still, try to obtain an old Ordnance Survey map of the area before it was flooded. This will show the prime fish-holding areas such as the original stream bed, sunken roads, buildings and other natural features such as trees and hedgerows.

Lastly, be confident and have faith in the method. Make trolling an important aspect of your approach to the sport and do not relegate it to a last resort when all else has failed. You are hardly likely to succeed with that outlook. Choose it at the right time and place and *it will* succeed for you.

Trolling Techniques

It is useless merely to pick any old lure, cast it somewhere astern and drag it behind the boat. Think about what you are doing and trying to achieve. Where are the fish most likely to be on the day? If you have a fish finder, check it out. At what depth are the baitfish shoaling and what areas do they normally frequent? Choose your lure accord-ingly and present it at a depth and speed most likely to appeal. This last point is of particular importance where perch are concerned. One day they will accept nothing

less than a lure fished at very high speed, whilst the next it must be almost inch-retrieved, so never be inflexible in your approach or take the fish for granted.

Slow trolling undoubtedly provokes the most takes but never overlook speed trolling when things are quiet. Short bursts of sustained throttle sometimes bring startling results – for example, the capture of two fish of almost three pounds each simultaneously on the same plug.

By speed trolling I mean just that. I have caught fish with a 4 hp outboard wide open. Make sure that your lure works with erratic diving movements when the throttle is jabbed open and shut. Don't worry about disturbing the fish either; they're probably totally oblivious of your topside antics some twenty feet or so above their heads. I expect this method sometimes succeeds so dra-matically because it creates an induced take, an involuntary reaction triggered by preda-tory instinct as the big, throbbing lure suddenly appears amongst the shoal.

In complete contrast, however, there are days when only the very slowest trolling speed will achieve results. One tip which comes in handy for slowing the boat right down is to drive it in reverse, literally steer-ing it stern forward. Other anglers may laugh at first but they'll soon change their minds when they bend into a big stripy.

Consider, too, how to take advantage of the elements, particularly wind direction. Obviously, motoring into a wind will slow the boat that much more than having the wind behind you. Drogues, used to good effect by trout anglers for certain styles of fly-fishing, can also slow you right down.

I often see anglers casting their lures well astern at the start of a trolling run. Why? If you simply lower your lure over the side of the boat and pay out line to the distance you require I guarantee that you will eliminate tangled traces or treble hooks locking with each other. You can also see the best speed at which to present the lure. What more could you ask?

Never leave the lure fishing for long periods without checking it periodically (say, every ten minutes). I am never happy unless I'm absolutely sure that my lure is not encumbered by weed and is fishing as effectively as I can make it. How often have you seen two anglers in a boat make a really tight turn while trolling a couple of lures? I see it all the time and I also see them having to untangle their crossed lines as a result. If you want to turn with two lures in the water make it a gentle curve. Indeed, if you steer the boat in a series of lazy S curves the baits dive rapidly and hover enticingly in alternate motions, thus increasing your chances.

Unless you are fishing a particularly shallow area, why have your rods pointing at the sky? Unless you are expecting the odd marlin to show up I suggest keeping the rod tip fairly close to the water – 30 degrees is about right to allow some movement in your rod if you wish to strike. Most authorities on trolling suggest speeding up the boat when a take is felt. This exotic pearl of wisdom was most probably handed down from someone who'd read a book on big-game fishing. When slow trolling, strike! Obviously, in speed trolling there are times when the momentum of the boat is sufficient for the fish to hook themselves, though this all depends on conditions on the day in question. I suggest, however, that you ignore any tiny plucks on the rod tip and wait for a good pull at all times.

Pete Rogers trolls in bright calm conditions on Ardleigh Reservoir.
Photo: Pete Rogers

Never guess how deep your lures are working. Know! Try them out beforehand and note it down somewhere if you are likely to forget. Why not mark the depth on the plug itself, in the same way that shot patterns are printed on floats? Having done this, make sure that you are fishing the correct or most likely combination of colour and action at the taking depth or where the highest concentration of baitfish can be seen on the fish finder. Remember too to vary the speed of the boat in accordance with water temperature. The warmer the weather the faster the metabolic rate of the fish, and so a faster presentation may be appropriate; the reverse, of course, applies when the weather cools.

If your highly prized and valuable lure gets snagged, don't lean into it with brute strength hoping this will do the trick. Stop, turn the boat, get right over the obstruction and handline it free. If this doesn't work, try pulling from different angles or try sending a device called an otter down the line attached to a strong rope, to snag the obstruction itself, which with a bit of luck can then be lifted.

Incidentally, make sure the clutch on your reel allows line to be taken in the event of your getting hooked into a snag or a very big fish. It can be most amusing at times to watch the attempts of some anglers to free line from their reels when they get snagged, with their rods getting dragged further and further into the water.

Marker Buoys

This important equipment is overlooked by most boat anglers. Having found your fish on a trolling run, trying to relocate them can be most exasperating if you lose your bearings. My markers are made from blocks of polystyrene cut into a square-sectioned dumb-bell shape and painted fluorescent orange (*see* Fig 25). Wound round the core is

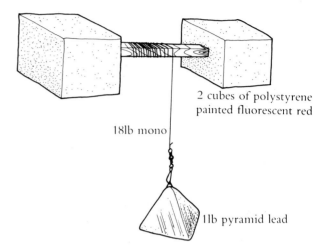

2 cubes of polystyrene
painted fluorescent red

18lb mono

1lb pyramid lead

Fig 25 'Dumb-bell' trolling marker.

plenty of 18-pound nylon attached to a 1-pound pyramid sea lead, which flips the block over and over like a waterwheel until the bottom is found. The shape of the buoy prevents further line spilling off. Two of these markers are used in lining up a trolling run as it is quite amazing how far you can drift when trolling very slowly in a stiff breeze (*see* Fig 26). I suggest that the person controlling the boat has them stored neatly and at the ready for when a shoal of fish is located, whereupon they can be dropped gently over the side.

Motors

If your boat is powered by a modern two-stroke petrol engine you are fortunate indeed as it will offer you economy, a fair turn of speed and a steady tick-over for reasonably slow trolling. If, however, you have to rely on a pair of oars then I would seriously recommend that you save your pennies and buy an electric trolling motor. Rowing about all day in a stiff breeze soon loses its novelty value.

An electric motor can be used on some reservoirs which prohibit petrol engines, and the joy of its quiet, simple and fume-free operation will make you wonder why more anglers do not own one. Whilst their battery life is limited and their power reduced, on the whole their convenience and ease of transportation easily outweigh the disadvantages. Of the various models currently available, my own choice is the American Minn Kota, which offers an infinitely variable throttle control and a gadget called a 'maximiser' which effectively prolongs the life of the battery. Obviously, the facility to increase or decrease the speed of the boat to vary the speed of the lure is a great advantage when trolling.

Finally, make sure that you buy a heavy-duty caravan or boat battery to power the motor. Unlike a conventional car battery, these are designed for regular charging. They also incorporate a carrying handle. Those of you who have manhandled car batteries any distance, spilling acid all over the place, will immediately appreciate this little bonus.

Fish Finders and Echo-Sounders

Whilst echo-sounders are most certainly a very useful piece of equipment for mapping out a water, I would advise anyone wishing to take up serious trolling to invest in a fish finder.

I do not intend to discuss the ethics of using this piece of equipment; rather, I suggest that you consider its merits when faced with limited fishing time on a huge expanse of water. I consider my time at the waterside all too important to be needlessly wasted and the use of a fish finder simply helps to cut down on this wasted time by telling me where *not* to fish. It is no substitute for the angling skill necessary to catch the fish once you have found them.

American anglers have been using these devices for many years and are so far advanced in the area of boat fishing that they make our own efforts look primitive. If you wish to

follow their advice I can only suggest that you go out of your way to obtain copies of their fishing magazines and books, particularly *In-Fisherman*. It really is an eye-opener.

From my own experience I can thoroughly recommend the range of Lowrance fish finders now available in this country. I haven't used the Humminbird range but these also appear to be very good. My own finder features an LCD (liquid crystal diode) screen forming hundreds of tiny squares (pixels) which in turn produce a picture of the area of water below the boat, showing bottom contours, tree stumps, weed and so on – and of course any fish in between there and the surface, which appear as blobs of varying sizes. There are a multitude of other functions the instrument can perform, such as finding thermoclines and magnifying the bottom, but I find the automatic function quite sufficient for my purposes.

PR

FISH RETENTION

Perch and keepnets do not go together, and this is especially true on reservoirs where they may have been brought up quickly through over thirty feet of water. Remember what I said earlier about their swim bladders. Large perch are only too prone to 'gassing up' when brought to the surface from this depth. Any big fish caught over deep water should be returned immediately to give it a fighting chance of survival.

If you must use a keepnet, then use the longest possible and first place a heavy weight inside to take it straight down. *Never* use a keepnet or other retaining device (for example a sack) if your boat is constantly moving, as you will simply drown your catch. Better to leave the net secured to a buoy and take the fish over to it. In my experience, however, it is not necessary to retain fish for long periods and the im-

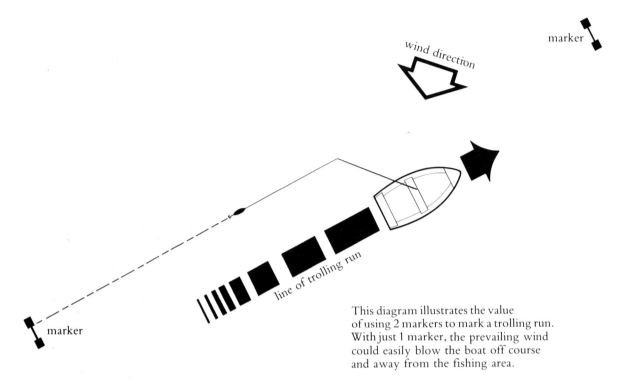

marker

wind direction

line of trolling run

marker

This diagram illustrates the value of using 2 markers to mark a trolling run. With just 1 marker, the prevailing wind could easily blow the boat off course and away from the fishing area.

Fig 26 The use of trolling markers.

mediate release of a fish will not disturb the rest of the shoal.

THE FUTURE

Sadly, the Bewl Bridge perch are no more. The water was struck by the perch disease in 1985 and the stocks have never recovered, and the same appears to have happened in the other southern reservoirs, Weirwood and Ardingly, both of which also lost their entire perch stock at around the same time. However, perhaps as a result of geographical and climatic differences, a large number of the trout reservoirs in the north and Midlands have escaped the disease and still hold prime stocks of great perch. At the time of writing Draycote Water is known to hold a huge

head of perch running to well over three pounds, though I do not believe that coarse fishing is allowed there at present. As time progresses, though, I believe that water authorities must face up to the fact that the day of the true mixed fishery, where coarse fishing can begin at the end of each trout season, is long overdue. Surely the additional revenue would more than compensate for the loss of a few trout – most of which (the rainbows) don't overwinter anyway.

With the apparent decline in our rivers, coupled with a recent increase in the numbers of people taking up fishing, it is obvious that the future of our sport lies in these great man-made waters, where the perch, the most beautiful of all our fishes, thrives so splendidly.

Shallow–Water Piking:
The Broads, Rivers and Lakes

It was overcast, mirror-calm and strangely mild for early February. Charles Beane and I had started on the river at dawn but as the morning progressed, it became much too busy for our liking and we finally decided to move to somewhere quieter and more secluded. Exploring within the vastness of the Thurne system can often turn up the odd surprise and so it did on this day as we quietly paddled the boat in and out of the tall Norfolk reed beds. Finally, we came across a large irregular-shaped bay surrounded and hidden by walls of reed and dotted with coot and duck which cautiously moved deeper into the bay as we silently drifted in.

The very shallow water was crystal-clear and broken with many lonely reed outcrops. We could easily see the uniform bottom for yards in all directions, even without polaroids. It was only inches deep (we later measured it at 22 inches) and lightly weeded in dark, irregular patches. I remarked to Charles that I didn't particularly fancy the area and we pondered awhile, watching the retreating wildfowl and scanning the still surface for any signs of fish. Eventually, out of habit, we decided to play safe, just in case, and give it a cursory half an hour. The thin line between success and failure had been crossed – for once in the right direction.

We tied up to one of the small reed outcrops about six feet from the main reed bed and fanned out our livebaits and deadbaits in all directions. Within only ten minutes, a float-paternostered livebait that I had cast into a narrow channel between two reed beds had been disturbed. An enormous heave of water, the ripples spreading slowly outwards, disrupted the mirror-calm surface until they finally died against the reeds on both sides. But the float remained stationary on the surface and I pulled gently back on the line to feel if the bait had been taken. It seemed to come free from light weed and the livebait once again tapped at the small streamlined float. But only for an instant. Again the water heaved. Not a swirl, nor a splash – no part of the fish visible. The water just seemed to lift upwards as ripples again spread across the channel. An obviously large pike was successful, at the second attempt, in finding its prey.

I imagined the underwater drama unfolding as the hunting pike stalked its quarry, moving in fast for the kill only to be thwarted at the last moment as the livebait dived for cover, burying itself in the soft, encompassing weed. The pike would probably have patrolled the edge of the weed bed, even probing into it at certain places, hoping to flush out the unfortunate roach from its sanctuary. My pulling back on the line had given it that second chance and this time there was no mistake.

The size and nature of the vortex had already indicated to me that this was no ordinary pike, so, after the initial sensation of heavy weight, I was ready for the sudden loss of pressure to the rod and reeled frantically to regain it as she ran in towards the

Stephen Harper cradels a thirty caught in less than 2 feet of water.

boat. The arc of the rod returned alarmingly at the last moment as the fish battled on, bow-waving past the back of the boat, charging through the narrow, weeded six-foot channel between the main reed bed and the small clump of reeds that we had tied up to.

Once it was through the channel and into open water I soon regained control; the fight was now less spectacular, and, after one abortive attempt at netting by myself, she obligingly headed nose first into the net and was secured by Charles. At thirty pounds three and a half ounces, I didn't mind if the battle had been brief, so long as it ended with that beautiful monster safely in the net.

I certainly learnt from the capture. Never again would I feel a lack of confidence fishing the extreme shallows in February, even if they did look bare.

After the episode on the shallows it occurred to me that no depth, or rather lack of it, can possibly deter even large pike as long as the water is deep enough to cover their backs. The angler may be deterred, his confidence fast slipping away as he sees the bottom for a considerable distance all round. But fish are masters of disguise, especially pike, which blend with their surroundings even in little or no cover. The only certain way to discover if you will catch in the shallows is to fish them. After all, at certain times of the year it is the shallowest areas that hold pike in numbers. They move in to spawn or to follow other species which are spawning, for an easy feast.

In British waters it is rare to fish in depths of more than twenty feet. Many broads, rivers and lakes are rarely deeper that ten feet and the majority of pike fishing is carried out at much lesser depths. A great deal of piking in and around Norfolk is practised in depths of less than eight feet, which I think can be accurately classed as shallow-water piking.

WHICH BOAT?

The choice of boat for these waters is less critical than on the inland seas of reservoir, loch or lough. Although some of these waters – Horsey Mere and Hickling Broad, for example – are vast sheets of water, their lack of depth and the surrounding flat countryside's moderating effect on the weather make fishing them an altogether much safer proposition.

A flat-bottomed, straight-sided wooden rowing-boat or a fishing punt, both in the traditional Broads styles, are ideal for these waters and provide a much superior fishing platform to boats of fibreglass design. But wooden fishing boats in these traditional styles are fast disappearing, to be replaced by the cheaper, lighter and more serviceable, if less stable, fibreglass rowing-boats in all shapes, sizes, designs and even colours. In fact almost all types of boat have been pressed into service at one time or another by part-time (or desperate) anglers, especially on the Broads. Canoes, yachts, sailing dinghies, and even cabin cruisers are all used throughout the busy summer and autumn season, but that is not to say that any of them are anywhere near suitable.

One of the best boats I have ever fished from was a wooden double-ended clinker-built shooting punt. Large and heavy but low-sided and a dream to row, its design meant that it cut through the water like a knife through warm butter, with little effort on the oars, and the low sides afforded little area for the Broadland winds to act upon.

A well-deserved 30 pounder for Martyn Page. Carpeting from the boat is also useful when photographing a large fish on the bank.

Where shall this bait be cast?

A pristine-conditioned 25 pounder from Norfolk's famous River Thurne lies almost completely across the well of Stephen Harper's punt.

The boat-yard at Ormesby had two such craft and I always made sure that I was there early as they were usually the boats to be taken out first. They must have been very old boats even by Broadland standards and sadly have long since been retired, replaced as always with the inevitable fibreglass.

Whatever type of boat is used, it can sometimes have one major effect on its occupant the moment he steps aboard. It can turn him into a *better* pike angler! That may sound strange, but some pike anglers do have very bad habits whilst bank fishing. These habits will always have an adverse effect on pike stocks, whatever the fishery.

For instance, some pikers stake their rods out along the bank at far too great intervals. And, once the morning has progressed with little or no action, our bored pikers will leave their rods to take a walk along the bank, sometimes even completely round the lake, to see how the other fishermen have fared. The result is inevitable – a deeply hooked pike. There is no way that this can

possibly be done whilst boat fishing, unless you have very high religious connections! A boat maketh a better pike man! On reflection, a bad pike angler on the bank is probably a bad pike angler in a boat, but at least one of his faults will have been removed.

LOCATION

The biggest problem to face any piker, experienced or inexperienced, on these shallow, featureless waters, and indeed any pike water, is finding the fish. Being at the top of the underwater food chain, these large predators are much fewer in number than the species of fish on which they prey.

Boats are the only answer to tackling the problem of location on these large waters. To take full advantage of their mobility, they should be used to cover as much water as possible until pike are contacted. Swim moves should be made at regular intervals of about forty-five minutes and are best carried out in a logical, methodical manner, using livebaits and deadbaits fished in a wide variety of different methods. Most broads, rivers and lakes are too large to cover completely in a day, so it is best to choose a manageable section and work it thoroughly in a grid, straight-line or zigzag fashion. If you skip sections that do not look promising, with sod's law in operation the chances are that these will be the areas that hold pike. If a plan is not adhered to, the pike concentrations will probably be missed.

On these sometimes very shallow waters, uniform depth can be a great hindrance to fish location. Any feature out of the ordinary is therefore of great importance. Bays, points, overhanging trees, snags, dyke entrances, feeder streams, even a slight change in depth should all be explored, with special attention paid to the areas not often fished – especially those lost and remote corners that have possibly never seen a bait.

Debate is often rife in piking circles about what areas of a broad are the most productive – the reed-fringed margins, as tradition dictates, or out towards the windswept central acres. There is no easy answer. On some broads, especially the very shallow ones, the slightly deeper centre is more productive. On the deeper broads, in particular those with depths along the shore-line, the margins can be the most rewarding areas. But there is no hard and fast rule for any water. All areas should be investigated to the full and conclusions formed by trial and error. Don't rely on local tradition; it can be very misleading, as pike do not take kindly to hard and fast rules.

A big Bure twenty taken on a float-trolled livebait.

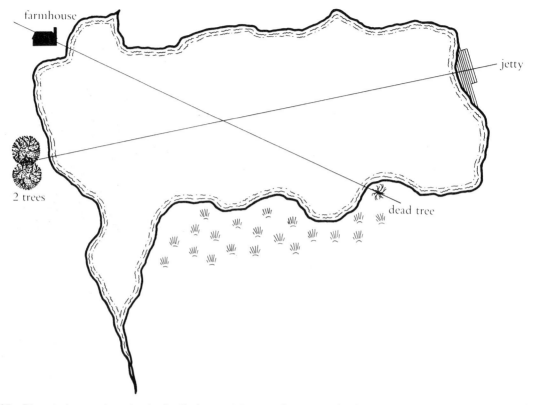

Fig 27 Pin-pointing a swim using bank-side features. Compass bearings make this technique even more precise.

Two other methods are particularly useful in locating pike. The first is to wobble dead-baits from a slowly drifting boat. This can only be done effectively in light winds, or with a drogue to slow the boat's progress in heavier winds. The boat starts upwind at the top of the broad, the angler or anglers wobbling deadbaits all around until the boat reaches the downwind shore. Then, after rowing back upwind, another drift is made over a completely different area. If fish are contacted, the anchors can be quickly lowered and the area fished in a conventional manner using all the usual methods and baits. Once you have located your quarry, pin-point your position by taking fixes on bank-side features.

FLOAT TROLLING

The second method is the float trolling of livebaits or deadbaits from a moving boat. It is probably the most effective method I know for locating pike and inducing them to take. Some anglers prefer to call this method 'trailing', but ever since it was popularised – first by Peter Butler in the late 1960s and then on Norfolk waters in the 1970s – it has been known as 'float trolling' and the term has now received widespread acceptance.

The method was not new even in the 1960s. The earliest reference I know of can be found in A. J. Rudd's delightful little book called *Fishing in Norfolk Waters,* in which he mentions the method used on the River Bure at Wroxham, which even to-day is an area renowned for float trolling.

A fish is netted in the wind-swept acres of Broadland.
Photo: Martyn Page

A large-headed Thurne pike of 27lb 9oz that engulfed a sunken float paternosterd live roach and ran straight in towards the boat.
Photo: Charles Beane

This book was first published in 1928, proving that in angling, nothing is ever original.

Float trolling, in its most effective form, calls for little or no wind, no boat traffic, no other anglers in the area, no snags and, on rivers, no fast currents. As these ideals rarely occur, it can be appreciated what hard work float trolling can be, but sometimes the rewards of hard work vastly outweigh the inconvenience.

Twelve-foot compound-taper rods and multiplier reels set on loosened ratchets are the ideal tools for the job. Terminal tackle is the usual two-treble rig and sometimes even a single lip-hooked treble.

The livebait or deadbait is rigged pointing up-trace and is usually of a smallish size, as missed runs can occur with larger baits. This may be because the pike has actually to double up the trace as it tries to swallow the bait head first. A small streamlined float is set overdepth and rigged as a slider. The angler can then increase the speed of the boat, raising the bait (through the float) off the bottom to avoid known snags or depth changes. A depth finder here can be very useful. A fair amount of non-toxic weight is sometimes needed to keep the bait well down and usually takes the form of a drilled bullet, resting above the trace or from two to four swanshot nipped onto the trace along the twisted area below the swivel.

The two rods, mounted in outriggers and fished at right angles to the gunwales, will help to keep the baits well apart. I have recently been working on a new float design that will also solve the same problem. These floats actually guide the bait either to the right or the left, thereby distancing it from the other float, tackle and bait, which are guided in the opposite direction.

The distance the baits are trolled behind the boat may be governed by weather conditions and finicky pike but it is often advantageous to troll one bait closer to the boat than the other. If a pike is indecisive with the first bait, he may take the second. I have never found one particular speed to be essential to success – as slowly as is practicable is usual. The main secret in the method is to cover a vast amount of water and, one hopes, many pike.

A customised pike boat really comes into its own when a take occurs, especially if you

Martyn Page with an 18 pounder taken on a bright and busy day on the River Bure.

A jack is expertly dealt with by Chris Turnbull.

Silhouetted against the early morning sun, the angler strikes into a pike in the boat-yards at Wroxham. A boat has been used here to reach an otherwise inaccessible bank.

are fishing alone. As soon as the ratchet on the multiplier signifies a take, the oars, tied to the rowlocks or with retaining collars or pins, can be totally disregarded. One of the anchors, already hanging outside the boat with its cable secured in a cleat, can be lowered silently on its pulley and the angler is ready to deal with the run immediately in the conventional manner. With two anglers aboard – one on the oars, the other manning the rods – the procedure is even easier, but with a well-prepared and equipped boat even the lone angler can be ready to strike that pike run almost immediately.

Livebaits have proved more effective than deadbaits but that probably reflects the fact that they have been used much more often. Now, on waters that see a lot of float trolling, the pike have to some degree wised up to livebaits, and a float-trolled herring or smelt has proved very effective.

Float trolling on the right water and in the right circumstances can be a real killer of a method. Its unique effectiveness in locating pike can be utilised in two ways: first as a preliminary to conventional, stationary methods; and second, and most importantly, as a fish-catching method in its own right. This is illustrated by the fact that often, once fish have been found by trolling, fishing the swim in the usual stationary manner produces no more takes. A return to float trolling the same area once again brings immediate success.

TIMES AND WEATHER

On these large expanses of shallow water it is important to keep one step ahead of the pike – and the other pike anglers. Each season on many waters, especially the rivers, pike head for certain areas in great numbers at particular times of the year. Their reasons are numerous and often not altogether clear, but knowledge of the migratory hot spots is half the battle in consistently catching pike. It is the anglers who know these areas and take notice of the trends who are the most consistently successful.

Many anglers pursue the pike from dawn until well into dusk. As the pike season commences, a dawn start is absolutely essential, and on a long autumn day sport is often over by 10 a.m., until, perhaps, the evening. As autumn creeps towards the long winter months, the dawn is not such a critical period and the pike do not become active until 9 or 10 a.m. Sometimes in the depths of winter this first feeding period can be as late as midday. But mornings generally are a much better proposition than the afternoons. Of course, large fish are caught at other times but my angling diaries over sixteen seasons in pursuit of pike show that mornings easily come out on top as the most productive fish-catching times of the day. There will always be a broad or a section of river to confound this observation and it should be recognised that, just as

there are morning waters, there are also some which habitually fish better in the afternoons. Realising which are which can be highly beneficial!

In my opinion weather is a minor consideration on these waters compared with fish location. Pike can be caught in almost any conditions imaginable, though on shallow waters the effect of the weather is more immediate. But I usually plan my pike trips well in advance and it is rare to cancel them because of adverse weather. Wind or frost may persuade me to change to a more suitable water, and in strong winds I might choose a tree-lined river to be able to float troll efficiently.

But occasionally everything falls into place. The weather is ideal, overcast and mild with a slight breeze rippling the surface. The boat is anchored over a vast shoal of feeding pike, both large and small. The company is good and the day is young with unfished acres all around just begging for attention and not another boat in sight. Heaven! Reward at last for those long fishless hours and hard work, for boat fishing is certainly that. Reward indeed for the hard-earned in-depth knowledge so indispensable even on these shallow waters.

The Deep Waters of the Loughs: Boat Fishing for Ireland's Pike

by Neville Fickling

Neville Fickling has dedicated his life to angling. By profession a fisheries inspector for the Severn Trent Water Authority, he has fished for pike since 1963. In that time he has amassed a staggering tally of twenty- and thirty-pound pike (topped by the Thurne fish of forty-one pounds six ounces) possibly unequalled in this country today. These fish have come from a vast variety of waters, many of them from the loughs of Ireland.

Along with his wife, Kathy, he organises membership and the finances of the National Association of Specialist Anglers and has recently taken on the role of secretary of the Pike Anglers' Club – a dedicated man indeed! Author of Pike Fishing in the Eighties *and* In Search of Predatory Fish, *he regularly contributes to the angling press. Although his main interests lie with the predatory fishes, he does enjoy 'dabbling' after the other species.*

In the following pages Neville offers some sound advice and words of warning to the angler afloat on Ireland's turbulent loughs in search of their legendary pike.

SH

The angler who is used to messing about in boats on the majority of English waters could well find himself out of his depth in Ireland. There is a world of a difference between even a 400-acre lake or broad and an Irish lough. You are attempting to fish a piece of water which can take on many of the characteristics of the sea – the waves can be very large and the rocks are not always obvious. At sea the boat angler usually has the benefit of a sea-going boat, a good Admiralty chart and, often, sophisticated aids such as sonar and radar. Yet time and time again English anglers think they can tackle a big water with the same boat they would use on English waters. Luckily no one I know has come to grief yet, but Germans in particular are very prone to underestimating a water, to such an extent

that Lough Allen has claimed one or two of them in the past few years.

WHAT TYPE OF BOAT

Accepting that the object of going to Ireland is to catch big pike and live to talk about it afterwards, what should we look for in a boat? First, within certain limits the bigger the boat the safer you are in heavy weather. A large boat will ride the waves better than a small one, which runs the risk of being caught in a trough and swamped. So to start with, the minimum safe size is about 16 feet, with 17- and 18-foot boats fairly common on most Irish waters. This generally rules out the idea of towing a boat that is normally used on the Broads to Ireland. Boats

'You're not going out in that are you?' 'Too right I'm not!'
Photo: Neville Fickling

Neville Fickling's first Irish twenty, 21lb 12oz taken on a trolled bait.
Photo: Neville Fickling

of 12 and 13 feet are worth taking only if you are fishing waters of similar size to those in England. So unless you can buy a boat and tow it, or keep it in Ireland, you are going to have to hire one. In many areas of Ireland the traditional boat is clinker-built and made of wood. My experience suggests that glass-fibre boats are just as good if not better. I have certainly felt safer in a good glass boat compared with a good wooden one. In terms of the amount of maintenance required, glass beats wood hands down.

I have no experience of cathedral-hulled dories, but quite a lot are used at sea so they must be worth considering. Their big advantage is stability, having a flatter bottom than conventional boats.

Boats fitted with thole-pins are initially harder to row than those fitted with row-locks. However, once you get used to them, or develop bigger muscles, they are prefer-able when you do need to row hard. Row-locks do not allow you to pull quite so hard, unless they have bars over the top, with the oars set permanently in them.

Power

The vast majority of boats are powered by petrol-driven outboards. I have used a few in my time, but at the moment the Yamaha and Mariner 4 seem to fit the bill. An out-board of this size on a big boat leaves you slightly underpowered, but there is a limit to the size of engine you can get in the car along with all the other gear. Some time I will invest in a 6-hp unit, which is probably about right. It takes over an hour to get from one end of Lough Allen to the other with a 4-hp and any aid to reducing travelling time is welcome. I'm a great believer in buying outboards new, the moral being that you will treat it well from the start, whereas a previous owner may have run it on the wrong mixture or otherwise mistreated it.

Always take spare shear-pins (or springs where fitted) in case you ground the prop. A shear-pin or spring is made of soft metal and breaks before any damage can be done to your gear train. Replacing it is simple, but you'll need pliers and spare pins or springs and split pins. You might also find a plug spanner and a spare plug useful. Plenty of fuel is obvious!

THE NATURE OF THE LOUGHS

The waters you are fishing will generally be large, and, because of this, location of the pike will be one of the biggest problems facing you. All Irish waters are fairly un-productive and certainly nowhere near as rich as some of our lakes. Because of this, food fish tend to be scattered around in shoals rather like currants in a cake. These shoals also tend to move around a lot. If you think this is a problem for us, pity the poor pike, who in order to make a living must find some food fish from time to time. Lough pike employ two main strategies to obtain food: they either wait at a good ambush point for some unfortunate fish to pass by, or they go looking for food fish and, having found them, try to stay close long enough for a successful capture to be made. Since the average pike only needs about three times its own weight of food in a year, it is clear that it does not have to be that good at catching food. For much of the time it won't be feeding, either because it is not interested or because it is full.

Our problems are therefore magnified. We have relatively few prey fish and even fewer pike, which are either sitting in key areas or on the move. Not all are hungry. So, if you approach an Irish lough as you would your local water and fish static with a few moves during the day, what are your chances of finding fish? The answer is, not very good. This is why trolling is a very

Homeward bound.
Photo: Neville Fickling

Measuring a large pike in the close confines of a boat can sometimes be no easy matter.

It is frequently easier to photograph a big pike on the shore. Ian Greenacre with a beauty of 23lb.
Photo: Neville Fickling

20 pounds exactly to a trolled copper spoon.
Photo: Neville Fickling

useful method, particularly for pike which are prepared to move to intercept a fast-moving bait. The theory is that if you pass a bait across enough pike during the course of the day you will sooner or later find a feeding fish. All you have to do is get it to take, hook it and land it!

During the spring, when the pike move into shallow water to spawn and then to feed on other fish also moving in for the same reason, trolling is of course generally impractical. At this time fishing from a boat in a static manner can be very effective. Generally spring pike fishing can be conducted from the bank, but the boat still remains a most useful item, carrying anglers and gear to any spot they choose in a fairly short time. While you may be able to walk to many swims from the road, the odds are

that you will not be able to make moves easily and this can be a handicap, especially when the first choice produces no pike. The boat enables you to move quickly and so increases your fishing time.

ANCHORS AND OTHER ESSENTIALS

Anchors are very important, for several reasons. Firstly, an anchor enables you to fish in a static manner in the area of your choice. An anchor also enables you to stop the boat if you have hooked a fish while on the troll. Normally you can play and land a pike on the drift while trolling, but if the wind is strong you may not be able to get

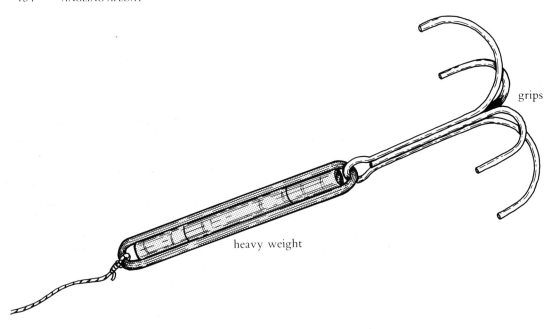

grips

heavy weight

Fig 28   The mega-anchor.

the pike to the boat. You may end up towing the pike behind. In this situation an anchor is essential. Similarly, if you are being pushed towards the shore while playing a fish you will need to anchor to avoid disaster. When there are two of you in the boat it is possible for one to hold station using the outboard. This eliminates the small risk of a pike tangling with the anchor rope.

For stopping a big boat effectively you will obviously need a substantial anchor. Mine is home-made and is made in two parts, a grip and a weight. The weight helps the grip to take a good hold. So far, luckily, the anchor has never become snagged, but this is always a possibility. A weak link, as described in Chapter 2, could easily be incorporated. There are several types of commercially available easy-release anchors, but few are big enough to do the job. It is easy enough to obtain a variety of anchors, simply by visiting a ships' chandler. Home-made anchors require a blacksmith or someone who is handy with welding gear.

For holding in shallow muddy bays the

oft-used mud weight, of 28 pounds, is ideal. Do not try using a 56-pound weight – you'll give yourself a hernia! Concrete mud weights are bulky and not usually heavy enough. To moor the boat you will require two, one at each end. Ropes should be braided if possible and not too thin, otherwise you'll have a job pulling the weight or anchor up. Needless to say, the Americans have motors to lift anchors; we will have to make do with brute force and ignorance.

Inside the boat, the obligatory piece of carpet or weighing sling cum unhooking mat is required to protect the pike. Trolling rests are useful if you are fishing two rods while on your own. I prefer to hold one rod so a rest can be used for the second rod. For static fishing, boat rod rests are not really required, because there is usually ample room to lay the rods across the boat. I will not give the usual lecture on tidiness in a boat, simply because I am terribly untidy. What is essential is to have a clear area to deal with the fish. Nothing damages fish more than thrashing around amongst sundry objects.

Another essential piece of equipment for fishing on these waters is an echo-sounder. Today you can buy ones such as the Seafarer D800 with a digital depth read-out, which will work for about 100 hours on the internal battery supply. In the bad old days sounders used a lot of current, requiring a 12-volt car battery or endless numbers of 6-volt lantern batteries. The D800 costs about £80 and will keep you informed of all the depths you pass over but will not tell you where the fish are. If you dig deeper into your pocket and are prepared to pay about £200 to £400 you can buy LCD-display graph recorders which show bottom features and fish. Generally the more you pay the better the definition. I've just bought a Humminbird 4ID and hope to give it a try in Holland for the first time. Some people have made snide remarks about the use of such devices, but, though they may help you find food fish and pike, you still have to get the pike to take. Luckily, there are no short cuts in this game.

TROLLING: DEPTHS AND AREAS

Irish loughs are not all the same, though few of the ones I have fished are particularly deep. Lough Allen drops down to eighty feet in some places, with much of the lake less then forty feet. Corrib, on the other hand, at least where I have fished, is seldom more than thirty feet deep. All in all a depth of about fifteen to twenty-five feet is ideal for trolling and it is also where the pike are most of the time in the period from June to February. A sounder enables the angler to fish certain depth ranges and to locate interesting features. I have caught a number of big pike from the edge of an underwater plateau and an equal number from points which protrude out into the lough. On the sounder such features are pretty obvious, though not all will produce pike. It depends on whether or not fish are in residence and whether they are willing to feed.

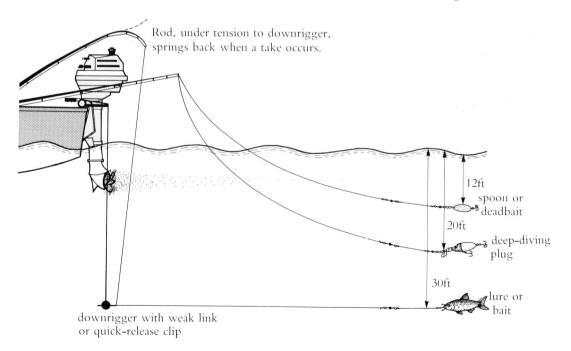

Fig 29 Trolling, with or without a downrigger.

Kevin Clifford prepares to lift out a small Irish pike by hand. The pike has different ideas!
Photo: Kevin Clifford

Trolling is usually carried out at tick-over on the outboard. It is possible to buy a cavitation plate to fit on the shaft, thus slowing the boat down further. This is worth considering if you are having to do a lot of trolling downwind, which can cause the boat to move a little too fast. I like to make use of the wind to slow the boat, although this may mean a fair amount of zigzagging in order to keep heading in one general direction. The depth at which you troll depends on where the fish are, but generally a lure or deadbait fishing at about twelve feet will take plenty of fish, because a pike will come up after a bait. To fish greater depths requires more lead, heavier spoons, or deep-diving plugs. As this is not a book on lure fishing I will not go into lure choice in detail, but it is wise to fish a lure and a deadbait at all times, since there is no guarantee which the pike will prefer on a given day.

To fish a lure consistently at, say, twenty to forty feet (something which is not usually called for) a downrigger is employed. This is a heavy weight which by means of a quick release clip enables the line and bait to be held at a predetermined depth. They cost from £50 to £100 and my next major invest-ment will be one of these.

However you choose to troll, it is useful to know how much line you have out, and a useful device called a Definder clips on the rod to tell you exactly that. Generally a lure or bait will be about thirty or forty yards behind the boat, so remember that snagging up will be preceded by plenty of notice if you are looking at the sounder. With trolled deadbaits I use stern-drag reels (mine are Daiwa GS2050BBs), and with the clutch set reasonably slack a take is quite audible. The lure rod is held and the takes usually hook themselves. On the deadbait rod, I give the pike as long as it takes to turn the boat back and tighten the clutch. An instant strike usually results in a missed take, so you must give the pike time to get the bait inside its mouth.

Trolling is something I always enjoy; the main advantage is that you are always fishing somewhere different. Static fishing is seldom as productive in the June–February period, unless you have located a big concentration of pike while trolling. Then, if you are near the bank of an island, it is possible to bank-fish. Otherwise you must anchor up, and this always seems so daunting, a tiny boat bobbing about in thousands of acres. Yet you can catch quite effectively if you have located pike. In the spring, boat fishing enables you to cover a lot of water during the course of the day, though for sheer comfort it is nice to be able to sit on the bank.

HOME COMFORTS

Over the years as I've grown older and less ready to rough it, a few little home comforts have found their way into the boat. An old plastic seat with no legs, found on the Thurne, gives back support on long days out on the water; I've just sent to the United States for a proper seat as used by the Americans so that should put an end to the sore-bum syndrome. If you can get a boat with a cabin or cuddy, then even better, because Ireland is one of the wettest places I have ever fished. Even the best clothing eventually fails against Irish rain. I like the Bob Church one-piece suit, but they do wear out very quickly if you do a lot of fishing.

A life-jacket is essential and you are irresponsible to go out without one. I generally wear mine only when the weather is in doubt; at other times it makes a good seat cushion!

THE ATTRACTION OF IRELAND

What then can the English pike man expect in Ireland? Surprisingly, the fishing is not generally that prolific. Frequently I have spent a week in Ireland for less than half a dozen double-figure pike. I could catch those in a day on some local waters. However, the attraction of Irish fishing is the known potential of many waters to produce pike of over thirty-five pounds, with the hope of something even bigger. The scenery takes some beating and of course there are the fighting qualities of the pike. I'm not sure which fight the hardest, Scottish or Irish pike, but either way be prepared to encounter something that will try to pull you out of the boat. That does not happen very much in England. So far I've been fairly lucky in Ireland. I have fished there about fourteen times and on only two trips did I fail to return with a twenty pounder. Like anywhere else, fish of over twenty-five pounds are not common, but if you are stuck in England fishing waters with limited potential then it is well worth going across the Irish Sea and giving it a try.

Each big fish you catch will remain etched in your mind, particularly if you have hooked one in eighteen feet of water. My first Irish twenty, twenty-one pounds twelve ounces, took a trolled trout and was not inclined at all to come up to the surface to see what was going on. On the minus side there are many days when boat fishing would be foolhardy and I have known people suffer a whole week of gale-force winds when the only prospect was to bank-fish somewhere. Problems such as wind cannot be avoided and one has to look at Irish pike fishing as a long-term venture. If you are willing to go regularly, you will eventually catch some good fish. One year will be brilliant, another poor. It is very much a case of taking the rough with the smooth. When you have fished there once, I'm afraid it can get to become a habit!

The Wild Lochs of Scotland

by Gord Burton

Gord Burton's enthusiasm for the sport of angling is contagious. His adventures with lures and Lomond are legendary, and he is one of the few pikers who fish the Scottish lochs all year round.

He has caught pike at depths of more than forty feet and he believes ardently that pike in excess of 40 pounds exist at those depths. Gord has specialised in trolling the depths of the lochs usually ignored by the vast majority who pursue Scotland's pike.

His knowledge and experience of the fish and the weather conditions on these sometimes wild waters is second to none and he has very outspoken and sometimes controversial views regarding all aspects of the Scottish lochs and the pike that inhabit them.

SH

Conditions, and therefore your approach to boat fishing, on the lochs of Scotland vary considerably according to the size of the waters. Some are less that 100 acres in size but many, including those I like to fish most of all, are much larger – mighty waters miles in length and width, thousands of acres of windswept vastness.

Fishing afloat on the smaller lochs does not pose any great problems as they are not subject to such changing weather conditions as are the huge waters.

Preparation is of the utmost importance when setting out to tackle vast sheets of water such as Loch Lomond and Loch Awe. A boat that may be suitable for fishing on a small lake would not be adequate for these lochs. In fact I've fished on numerous waters from boats that I wouldn't dream of venturing out on Lomond in. I shall concentrate on Lomond since the experience I have gained there is enough to enable an angler to venture onto any water and overcome any problems or hazards.

Most important of all is knowing the capabilities of your boat and being satisfied that it will sail through the very wild weather you may get caught out in. It must also be a robust enough craft to withstand scrapes from rocky reefs and getting knocked about when being beached on stony shorelines. I have fished on the big lochs throughout the course of a whole year and it is surprising how much the weather and water conditions change as the seasons progress. The water level can vary as much as ten feet between summer and winter. Areas I have fished during the early and later months of the year may almost dry out during the warmer periods of summer.

ROCKS AND REEFS

One year I saw all of the shallows from the Endrick Bank and Crom Mhin Bay on Lomond completely dry up as the level of the loch dropped very low indeed, and during this period many rocky hazards revealed themselves. Around many islands

The boat-yard at Balmaha on Loch Lomond in early spring.
Photo: Gord Burton

and along the shorelines are large areas of rocky and boulder-strewn ground. There are long reefs of jagged rocks just jutting from the surface for a foot or so, but when the rains come and the levels begin to rise these perilous objects may be covered by only inches of water. If the boat fisher is not familiar with such hazards, and motors into an area of rugged ground, imagine what might happen in a collision with a big sharp-edged boulder. The boat could be badly holed, flooded out and barely float. Worse still, it might sink. I have seen such occurrences many times. Take great care where you motor your boat.

Before venturing on these big lochs, study maps and charts of the water. An echo-sounder is an *essential* piece of equipment. It will tell you when you are over shallow water, when you must motor along very slowly. On Loch Lomond rocks abound around Inch Cailloch, Clairiach, Inchtavannach and Aber Isle, and all along the southern shoreline, Ross Priory and Portnellen. On Loch Awe the areas around Inishail and the Black Islands are very dangerous, as also is the area adjacent to the Kilchion Castle at the top end of the loch.

By no strange coincidence, these places of danger are also noted hot spots for big pike.

WILD WEATHER

Over years of fishing in Scotland, as well as some time in Ireland, I have experienced all possible conditions short of a hurricane, and I'm not telling stories. At times I have fished through day after day of torrential rain, which floods the inflowing rivers and spews dirty water into the loch. This can seriously affect the fishing. During one four-day session

This photograph was taken from exactly the same spot as the previous picture but during the winter floods.

Photo: Gord Burton

on Lomond it never stopped snowing; in fact snow-ploughs had to be brought out to open the road out of Balmaha. Once a pea-souper of dense fog came down as I was motoring across the loch and I was lost. I had no compass in my tackle box and it was only when a haze of sunlight showed up in the sky that I could motor straight at it and find the shoreline, following it back to base. Since that day I've always carried a compass and have crossed lochs in dense fog on many occasions.

These big lochs are well known for sudden squalls that whip up in no time. A fresh wind can increase to a raging gale in a very short time. I wouldn't like to be caught in a little lightweight craft two miles out on Lomond when it suddenly turns angry. It sounds strange, doesn't it, talking of being miles out on a water when pike fishing, but

that is how it is on Lomond. I have been caught out on the loch in a raging storm and had the boat bouncing and crashing through white-capped rolling waves. Finally, there have been times when I have had to smash my way through ice to get to open water when both Lomond and Loch Ken were, for the greater part, frozen over.

All of this sounds a little awe-inspiring. Some people have said that my mate and I must be mad to fish through such conditions, but since we had decided to tackle the big lochs the whole year through it was inevitable that all forms of weather would have to be endured. My boat *Creek Chub* has seen it through and we have gained much experience.

In comparison, the many smaller lochs such as Rutton, Milton, Loyne, Ken, Achty, Woodhall and many others – present no

Stephen Harper with a stocky Lomond 19 pounder.

Gord Burton likes the fish to put a bend in his rod. This fish was hooked on the troll. Note sturdy trolling rests and life-jacket.

Photo: Gord Burton

Another Lomond pike battles it out.

problems. Dense fog won't leave you thinking you could be stranded, you won't smash into rocky reefs a long way from shore and big gales won't whip the water into a seething cauldron.

After warning you of the hazards – and it's not always wild – I'll now come to the serious business of fishing in comfort and, most of all, in safety.

THE LOCHS: A DAUNTING PROSPECT

When faced with the prospect of fishing an immense sheet of water, the newcomer or even an experienced campaigner on lesser waters can be faced with a bewildering proposition. Gone is the sense of security and the knowledge that the fish can easily be found. Because Lomond and Awe are so vast, finding and catching pike on them in winter presents a real problem. The pike have a much wider choice of habitat, depth, and – in some instances – diet than on smaller waters. Apart from that, the fishing isn't difficult provided you are well prepared for the task in hand. It is certainly no Herculean task, as one misinformed writer once said of fishing on Lomond.

THE *CREEK CHUB*

Let's look at the most important thing, the boat. Mine is a 13 footer with a beam of over 5 feet and is deep from the gunwale. It is a real seaworthy craft that has been tested to the limit.

A lightweight fibreglass boat is no good on the big lochs when there is a fair chop on the surface. They lack stability and get thrown about too much and I've been seasick a time or two because of this. My boat has a lot of woodwork on its gunwales, seat, stern and transom. Besides this, I have two

wooden box compartments built into the gunwales, one on each side, specially for storing food, cooking utensils, and so on. Up front in the bows is where the gas bottle for the store is fastened. Whenever I go to fish in Scotland my boat is my base. It is where I sleep, eat and stay until it is time to return home. When I turn in for the night a large sheet completely covers everything from my cuddy to over the stern. Incidentally, always choose a nice sheltered bay to anchor up for the night, never out in the main loch, just in case the weather turns wild.

To combat the reefs and other rocky terrain, the bottom of my boat has been reinforced with a coating of fibreglass matting and resin over 2 inches thick in places. Because of this strengthening I have no fear of colliding with rocks or stony shorelines when beaching or when motoring in rocky areas. This extra fibreglass also adds stability, making my boat comfortable to fish from even in rough water.

Anybody with any amount of experience of fishing in Scotland will know all about wet weather because when it rains up north it can be very generous. Good waterproofs are essential if you are to fish as comfortably as possible. It is no good having wet weather conditions hamper your efforts when you have travelled a long distance to fish. A cuddy helps a great deal but suitable clothing is still needed. A good bailing can is also vital – it is surprising how quickly a boat can fill with rainwater.

During the years I've had my boat there have been many occasions when I have been caught out a long way from shore by a sudden storm or even a raging gale. Knowing the capabilities of the craft prevented me worrying about such conditions. So, most of all, before setting out to fish these places, select a good, stable boat. Something between 13 and 16 feet is ideal. I've fished from some lovely wooden clinker boats in the past and these are superb craft. If you have a fibreglass

Loch pikers have it tough at times. Gord Burton in a Lomond blizzard.
Photo: Gord Burton

dinghy, make sure it has plenty of weight around as ballast because a lightweight type gets tossed about far too much in a fair wave and fishing is uncomfortable. A boat along the lines recommended is ideal for any water the angler is ever likely to fish in British fresh water.

ENGINES, ANCHORS AND ACCESSORIES

On small lochs there is little need for an outboard engine but a motor is essential if the angler is to tackle big waters and get the best results from his efforts. Without one an all-round piker cannot work.

I travel miles from base when fishing Lomond, Awe and Loch Ken and often troll for pike for day after day, so a good reliable engine is very important. When all is said and done, I wouldn't want to have to row back to the landing base, which may be ten

miles away, especially if there is a wave on the loch. It would be very hard work, so a trusty outboard is a must. Seagull outboards and my Evinrude 6 have never failed me in all the years I've used them to push my boat along. The only mishaps have been broken shear-springs resulting from collisions with rocks, reefs or the bottom in shallow areas.

Another type of problem occurred when I left the air-intake screw open on top of the petrol tank during a long day of torrential rain. Water seeped into the fuel and turned it the colour of milk. The engine started with what was left in the carburettor but soon conked out. Luckily I had some clean spare fuel and made it back to base. Look after your petrol containers and ensure that they are kept dry. Always carry a small tool kit and spare shear-pins. Tie or chain your engine to the transom just in case the screw clamps work loose. Outboards have been known to come off and sink into the depths.

To keep my oars out of the way when

fishing, two short lengths of rope with nooses tied on them are set several feet apart along the gunwales, just below the tops but inside the boat. The oars are slipped through the loops and then hung over the edge, suspended over the water. Rowlocks can cling to an oar when it is being lifted up and then suddenly fall off, usually into the loch! To prevent this I've fastened a short length of chain to the end of the rowlock that slots through the gunwale and attached it to the woodwork. There is no danger of it falling into the water if it is lifted out. When not in use the rowlocks hang inside the boat and cannot get lost as they're chained down.

To hold the boat in a stable position when fishing, two mud weights are used. In the past I have tested all forms of anchors – paint tins filled with concrete, hessian sacks filled with loch-side stones, plough and other metal-wedge types. All of them do the job in certain situations but for precise position-ing there is nothing to beat a heavy steel mud weight. Mine were made by welding pieces of offcut scrap metal into a solid block weighing about forty pounds for my main holding anchor, and about twenty pounds for the stabilising weight. I attach a 3-foot length of chain to the heavy weight and this acts as a buffer and takes some of the pressure when a fair wind is blowing. The best type of anchor ropes I have used are those thick hemp types which lorry drivers use to secure their loads in transit. They are ideal and easy to grip when hauled up from what can sometimes be very deep water.

In my early days of fishing these big lochs I would never have imagined anchoring in up to sixty feet of water but experience has taught me that such a rope length is some-times required to hold a boat in a strategic position. In the past many pike have taken my bait between thirty and fifty-five feet down as I have trolled the deeps.

Once the mud weights are bedded in they will hold the boat in a stable position even when a fair wind is blowing. The main anchor is usually angled at 45 degrees away down from the bows of the boat but the stabilising weight is lowered straight down off the stern, alongside the outboard engine. I've also fitted a sheet of thin-gauge metal over the gunwale to protect it when the anchor is hauled up.

Other minor pieces of gear I keep in the boat are a few old cloths for cleaning up, wiping hands and cleaning the engine. They can also be placed over the stern of the boat to protect the rods and line when you motor to your fishing spot. A large sheet of carpet covers a good area of the deck of the boat to protect the bodies of big pike when they are hauled aboard. Not only that, it is also better to stand on and safer than wet boards.

SAFETY

I know of many fatal accidents on Loch Lomond and I once read in a Sunday news-paper that on average seven people a year drown in the loch. Even on small lochs I know of pike anglers who have drowned. Many, many times I have seen anglers motoring across Lomond wearing waders and heavy clothing but without a life-jacket!

Lomond and Awe are miles wide and if a gale capsizes the boat a long way from shore the angler could be in very serious trouble and even pay the ultimate price. It really surprises me just how thoughtless some anglers are when it comes to safety when afloat on such huge waters. Many times I have fished through wild weather and I have been caught out in horrendous gales, but I've always motored safely back to base without fear because I know the sailing capabilities of my boat *Creek Chub*, and I always wear a top-quality life-jacket. Experience and preparation now allow me to fish in comfort 90 per cent of the time but I hasten to add that this know-ledge was earned the hard way!

A 25 pounder with some impressive teeth, that took a liking to whole mackerel.
Photo: Gord Burton

AN APPROACH TO LOCH FISHING

Most of the anglers venturing onto the lochs of Scotland are experienced pike fishers so I won't go into too much detail about tackle set-ups but will give advice on how my mates and I approach our fishing.

Most of all, the angler must be versatile if he is to get the best results for the effort he puts in. Hot spots can vary from large areas of shallow water, with little in the way of snags, to shallow but very rocky spots. A very good holding area may be round the rocky outcrop of an island, and in such spots I have taken big pike on livebaits and deadbaits from depths ranging from a couple of feet to almost forty feet down.

Whatever position the boat is anchored in, I always present a bait deep down, and this will usually be a livebait. Another livebait will be positioned on a ledge higher in the water, and if three rods are being used then a deadbait will be fished on the shallowest ledge. This is because in my experience the pike patrolling such areas are usually on the prowl and are more likely to pick up a deadbait than one fished deep down.

To ensure consistent results the angler must use as varied a tactical approach as possible. Apart from all the standard methods of live- and deadbaiting, greased line and wobbling deadbaits are sometimes put to use, and, most of all, lure fishing. Through being versatile my mate Rob Forshaw and I have had some incredible catches of big pike – over 400 pounds of fish in a three-day session and over 600 pounds during a one-week trip.

Many times, when fishing has been slow, I have gone off in search of fish – casting plugs when at anchor, drifting over an attractive-looking area, or trolling long distances to locate a pack of pike mad on the prowl for food. One such session produced nearly 200 pounds of pike in a morning. Another short session brought nearly 140 pounds of mad, plug-champing, head-shaking demons.

For trolling, two sturdy rod rests (*see* photograph at foot of page 142) are clamped onto the gunwales and these enable me to motor through rough water without fear of the rods bouncing out of them. In many articles for fishing afloat on these lochs I have advised heavy tackle in comparison with fishing for pike in general. This isn't just because the big loch pike are exceptional fighting fish, but boat fishing is rugged going and your gear tends to get knocked about somewhat, so it pays to step up in strength and power.

FINAL TIPS

While you are fishing, keep everything in the boat ready for action. Have scales, unhooking gear and camera ready at hand for when a pike is boated. If you have hooked a big fish get the lightweight stabilising anchor lifted into the boat; these powerful pike will be underneath you at some time during the fight and with ropes down at each end of the boat the fish could swim round one and break off. Once the fish is boated get all jobs done. Photograph the fish in the boat. Don't up-anchor and go to the shore to take pictures – the big loch pike move in packs and being away from the hot spot could cost you more big specimens. Rob and I have had three big fish in the boat together when a pack of them have suddenly struck, so be prepared.

Fishing can be exceptional at all times of the year and being well prepared beforehand will greatly add to your enjoyment in these most splendid of surroundings. To me, this is the ultimate in pike fishing.

Safe piking!

Adrift on Inland Seas:
The Fishing Boat Abroad

by Martyn Page

In recent years Martyn has made numerous trips to the Continent and the United States. Business commitments with his tackle company, Marvic, have often provided ample excuse to travel and sample the exotic delights of angling abroad.

No mean angler on his home waters of Norfolk, he has big fish of most species to his credit, though pike remain a firm favourite. Indeed, from 1981 to 1985 he was first treasurer and then treasurer and secretary of the Pike Anglers' Club.

With John Bailey he co-authored the classic books Pike – The Predator Becomes the Prey *and* Carp – The Quest for the Queen *and is currently compiling a vast volume on pike with his partner in Marvic, Vic Bellars.*

But it is to overseas that he looks for new and different challenges for the future – a giant pike from Holland or a monster muskie from Minnesota. There is so much to be learnt from our foreign counterparts. Martyn's chapter provides pointers to how we can adapt their methods and fish with the advantages gained from angling that is in many respects years in advance of our own.

SH

We had fished the spot well and covered all likely areas. Doug observed that it was time for a move, and fired the outboard into action. Ten minutes later we settled in the next swim – some five miles away!

This was the beginning of our three-week introduction to fishing the huge lakes of the United States. During those weeks our eyes were to be opened to the fine arts of location and approach and a new way of thinking which was to eliminate the daunting aspect of tackling large inland seas.

Americans are notorious for gadgets, electronics, this, that and the other, and before our visit we were convinced that so much of their way of fishing was purely of a gimmicky nature. Now, perhaps, we can reflect on our experiences. It is true there are many gimmicks associated with the American way of sport fishing, but this is true also of our European styles.

America is about big lakes, fast, hard-fighting predatory sport fish such as pike, muskie, salmon and walleye, and, most importantly, quality fishing boats. These are boats made for the angler, perhaps costing over £1,000, laden with electrical gadgets, powerful outboards, electric outboards, graph recorders, and even swivel fighting chairs.

When you are out on an American water the nearest alternative swim may be several miles away. Oars therefore become impractical; instead, a high-powered outboard and streamlined speedboat is the order of the day. It takes only minutes to reach that

A Lowrance fish finder and downrigger winch – equipment for vast waters.
Photo: Martyn Page

swim travelling at 30 or 40 mph, bouncing across the waves – and I mean waves, for these are not waters for the faint-hearted. When the wind blows these seas really do roll and sea sickness tablets can save the day.

It is difficult to convey in words the size of some of these waters. For those who have fished Loch Lomond, suffice it to say that this is small in comparison. Take Lake Superior, for instance, a lake partly in America and partly in Canada, 31,820 square miles of fresh water (a tenth of the world's fresh water supply) full of great salmon, trout and pike, to name but a few species. Now that is a challenge!

THE AMERICAN APPROACH

Obviously, most American sport fishing is conducted from a boat. As will be apparent from my earlier comments, not only are these designed as fishing machines but they must also be extremely stable and designed with comfort in mind. However, whatever size the water, a boat is merely a fishing platform, a means of access, whether on a small Norfolk broad or out in the middle of Lake Superior. The Americans insist, in their outgoing way, on quality and added comfort, and who can blame them? Their approach, though, centres on the key to all fishing for predators, whether at home or abroad, and that is location.

We have much to learn from the Americans about fish location, particularly on our larger waters. Most competent anglers will soon get to grips with our average lakes and rivers but many are daunted by the prospects of tackling even our 'large' lakes and reservoirs, and even on Lomond anglers stick firmly to recognised 'safe' areas such as Balmaha and Ardlui.

There are few such sanctuaries on the

Vic Bellars with a large mouth bass taken from the comfort of a padded swivel chair on the Mississippi.

Photo: Martyn Page

American seas; it is a case of getting out and finding the fish. It is no good fishing a swim for an hour and then moving to the next in a slow grid search, for that would take a lifetime. Instead, an understanding of where the fish may be at a particular time of year is necessary, and the Americans have gone into this in a very deep, scientific and analytical way. They are years ahead of us with regard to fish behaviour, seasonal movement and location in such waters. Even so, their waters are so vast that they need electrical gadgets. There is no case for ethical questioning of whether such devices are sporting or not. Quite simply, on most of their waters your chances would be zero without them. To consider searching

a large water for predatory fish without a graph recorder is clearly a nonsense. At first we also thought that gadgets for determining temperatures at particular depths, or water and light conditions (in order to determine the best lure colour), were merely gimmicks. I soon began to change my mind.

The lesson of our American experience is that no water is too deep or too daunting. But you need a graph recorder, you need an understanding of where the fish might be, you need a good boat with a powerful outboard and you need to understand trolling techniques, with and without downriggers.

Duncan Kay heads out towards some distant swim in a large purpose-built American fishing boat.

Photo: Martyn Page

MANOEUVRING AND APPROACHING A NEW SWIM

Not only do Americans know how to find fish, they also know all about boatcraft. They may hurtle at 30 or 40 mph between swims, but they recognise the need for a silent approach so as not to disturb a shy old muskie. This is where the electric outboard comes in, and if you've seen an American using one of these with a foot control you will truly appreciate the quietness with which one can approach a swim. No noisy squeaks from rowlocks, clanks from oars or the noise of a normal outboard. Instead an almost inaudible hum, barely a ripple moving from the boat as it is edged forwards, backwards or sideways into the desired spot by means of a simple foot control. As he approaches, perhaps, a shallow plateau, the American angler still has both hands free to make a cast to the patrolling muskie, whilst keeping the boat firmly under control. It would be almost poetry in motion except for the fact that I still cannot reconcile such expertise and competence with the use of such short beanpoles, tow-rope fishing line and monstrous treble hooks. Perhaps there will always be room for improvement in all branches of angling.

On one occasion I was in a boat with Doug Stange. Vic Bellars was in a nearby boat with his American guide. The guide had a follow from a large muskie (twenty-five pounds plus) and, being an inquisitive beast, the muskie stayed with the lure even when the retrieve was finished. This is common with these magnificent fish and the American answer is to dip the rod tip into the water and move the lure, which has been reeled to within 18 inches of the tip, in a frantic figure-of-eight under the water. Often this agitates the muskie into taking and that is precisely what happened on this occasion. With clutch tightened (with a spanner), such a short beanpole and 40-pound line, something has to give when a muskie hits in this way. In this case it was the angler who struggled hard to avoid being pulled over the side. Believe me, this fishing can give some truly heart-stopping moments when such big fish are attacking right up against the boat.

On another occasion Doug was once more demonstrating his expertise with an electric outboard, as we wobbled baits for muskie on the Mississippi. Now that is one enormous river. We were fishing some 3,000 miles up-river from the sea and it was still several hundred yards across and had a pull which would probably have required a 6-ounce break-away for normal legering. Doug was slowly easing the boat downstream by means of the electric outboard and we were casting wobbled baits into slacks and eddies.

Despite the fact that the water was very coloured and more than twenty feet deep, it was necessary to keep the baits near to the surface and the muskie would appear as if from nowhere. On this occasion we were about to move downstream. Vic's retrieve was virtually finished and as he lifted his lure from the water, turning away, I saw a projectile rocketing vertically from the depths. Something in the order of thirty pounds of muscle took to the air in an attempt to capture its escaping meal. All I could do was shout for Vic to stop but it was too late. His bait had been taken from the water and the muskie crashed, disappointed, back into its sanctuary.

We were fishing in Minnesota and Wisconsin close to the Canadian border where there are thousands of lakes. Not all were such enormous lakes and often, as we were travelling a hundred miles or so to the next water, we would pass countless beautiful and inviting small waters of 100 acres or so. When we asked him what was in these

and whether they were worth fishing, Doug's reply was usually that they contained no fish as they completely froze in winter – not just the surface, the whole thing.

During another session we were using downriggers to troll Lake Michigan. It was a warm day and the salmon were well off-shore. We had moved five miles out and still very few fish were appearing on the graph recorder. I asked my guide – an Italian from Chicago, called Toni – how long before we reached the other side. His reply was that it was fairly narrow at that point and that there was only another 120 miles to go!

LESSONS FROM THE STATES

I learnt a great deal during those three weeks in the States. Not only did I gain confidence on such huge waters, including Lake Superior, I also began to understand the development and sophistication which the Americans have applied to the art of location of fish in their waters. This knowledge has led to a greater understanding of other large waters I have subsequently fished.

Naturally, I do not agree with all the American styles and, indeed, while we were over there our English techniques and Anglo-American adaptations raised a few eyebrows. The message is a strong one, however. When approaching a large water it is essential to be equipped with a proper boat – not one that would suffice on a small lake but one that will be stable and safe. In addition there are other essentials. Most of these are not cheap. For instance, a good graph recorder will cost several hundred pounds but when it means the difference between fish and no fish then surely the money is well spent. Then there is the electric outboard, possibly the most neglected piece of equipment by English and other European boat anglers. They are readily available over here; in fact Shakespeare market an excellent model. If it is stealth that you require, or more control over the boat for manoeuvring or trolling, the electric outboard is the answer.

A number of American techniques were totally new to me. The Americans are famous for their lure fishing, and perhaps the most significant development is the use of downriggers. I must say that I am not yet convinced. It is true that a downrigger can ensure that a bait is fishing at a specific depth, and in conjunction with the graph recorder, you can fish in the knowledge that the bait is at the same depth or just above the quarry. But the problems of a downrigger become apparent immediately after the take. For a period the line is slack as the clip releases. Numbers of fish seem to be lost at this stage. I suppose that if the downrigger results in a great number of additional takes the ratio of lost fish is acceptable. On most

Martyn Page proves that not all American fish from inland seas are gigantic!

Photo: Martyn Page

of our European waters, however, it is possible to troll baits at the required depth without resorting to their use.

Downriggers aside, lessons learned in America were invaluable, the experience was unforgettable and without a doubt that enormous country offers some of the most varied and exciting freshwater boat fishing in the world.

CLOSER TO HOME

Since visiting the States, Vic Bellars and I have been privileged to sample European pike fishing on some of their larger waters. They might not quite be the seas that we found in America, but nevertheless they are big waters with dramatic depth changes. Here location once more depends on the use of electronics, quality boats are necessary and trolling techniques tend to produce the greatest rewards. Pike run to huge proportions in these waters and many never see an angler's bait. We have been privileged to fish several waters in Holland in which pike of over forty pounds are caught every year and where sixties and even seventies are surely present, waters that have also produced twenty-pound-plus zander and five-pound-plus perch – the Cassiens of the predatory world.

Our lessons from America have helped and the guidance of such great pike anglers as Bert Rozemeijer has proved invaluable. These are the waters of the pike angler's dreams. He may not be able to afford America and the unique muskie, but these European waters lie just a short North Sea crossing away.

The large Dutch waters obviously each have their own specific characteristics, although noticeably they are usually extremely clear and deep. Bert has developed a style for trolling these waters which, although in itself extremely simple, is very

A downrigger in action on Lake Michigan.
Photo: Martyn Page

Closer to home, Martyn Page displays a Norfolk 20
pounder and attractive carpeting!
Photo: Martyn Page

intelligently thought out and designed to give maximum returns.

Basically, in such clear water, a feeding pike retains a high attack profile. This means that one can troll consistently at a depth of fifteen feet in the knowledge that the majority of large pike will be lying between fifteen and thirty feet and will attack upwards. Although we have managed to catch pike at depths up to sixty feet, they have invariably been small and Bert's findings over the years confirm that we were correct in our early conclusion that the larger pike generally do not lie at such depths. Effectively, the style used is to fish over the pike. There is little point in fishing under them – just look where a pike's eyes are set. With clear water,

even if you are fishing ten or more feet above the pike, if they are on the feed they will attack, rising from the depths to take the bait. Indeed, we have cruised over water 100 feet deep following a bream shoal swimming lazily across the surface and seen giant pike – twenties, thirties and larger – crashing into them.

The method is to use a graph recorder to troll the fifteen- to twenty-foot contour. One bait fishes five to seven feet shallower than the other. The graph recorder is not used to locate but to maintain this depth. A water where sudden drop-offs from ten to 300 feet occur requires a precision electrical instrument; the job cannot be done by memory or guesswork. At times, however, the graph recorder records awe-inspiring shapes, sitting angled and poised for attack.

There is little point in sitting anchored (if you have enough rope) for hours on end in a likely-looking spot. These are big waters and the philosophy is to cover as many pike as possible by trolling the key holding depths. In this way some feeding pike will be covered and certainly Bert's results over the years have convinced me that his style is one of the most efficient for these large waters.

The rig itself is simple: enough weight to hold a bait down, a large bait – either a big livebait of about 12 ounces or a large mackerel or other deadbait. Balsa is inserted into the back of the deadbait to ensure that it trolls on an even keel rather than head up in the water. There is no place for light lines with this fishing. Reel line of 18 to 20 pounds to 28-pound wire and size 4 or 2 hooks are called for. Obviously a relatively large streamlined float is needed to take such a bait and here we come to one of the major

refinements to standard trolling techniques. As one trolls with a sliding float, all too often the float itself has a tendency to slip slowly down the line, drawing the bait up to fish shallower. This can be totally overcome by the use of a bottom-end-attachment float, clipped to a small U-turn locking device, which is threaded on the main line. While there is no pressure this device allows the line to slip through it to the stop-knot. Once under pressure, because of the U-turn, the device locks and the float cannot slide down the line. As a result you can fish properly at the required depth in the certainty that the bait has not been drawn up to the surface.

One cannot fish a multitude of rods with this trolling method. One man on the oars

Vic Bellars, eyes fixed on the fish finder, float trolls one of Holland's vast freshwater lakes.

A Dutch zander that fell to a large, double-bodied plug.

and one in control of the two rods is sufficient. The hard work rests with the oarsman, who has to guide the boat along the contour, eyes constantly on the graph recorder. Outriggers can be used to keep more distance between baits but usually, as with most trolling techniques, one bait is fished farther from the boat than the other. All that is needed is a slow troll and some luck, and the dream becomes reality.

This is trolling in its simplest form, logically thought out and applied in a manner which ensures that a bait of the

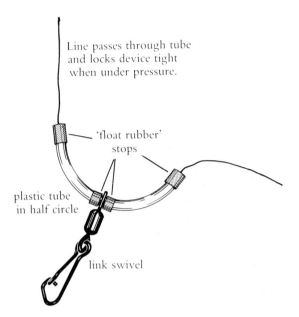

Line passes through tube
and locks device tight
when under pressure.

'float rubber'
stops

plastic tube
in half circle

link swivel

Fig 30 The 'U-turn' locking device.

correct size (remember that these are very abundant waters with a good head of quality baitfish) is drawn in front of the maximum number of pike. When the float dives away it is no wonder that the heart misses a beat as thoughts of fifty-pound pike run through the mind.

In conclusion, fishing some of the large European waters and American inland seas is the logical progression for the adventurous and ambitious angler. A little British island soon loses significance when you are faced with the superb sport fishing which can be sampled abroad. The techniques for tackling these inland seas are relatively simple and straightforward, aided by sophisticated electronic technology and, most important, the comfort and safety of a well-designed and fully equipped fishing boat.

Index